| DATE DUE | | | |
|---|---|---|---|
| JUN 08 '02 | | | |
| | | | |
| | | | |
| | | | |
| | | | |
| | | | |
| | | | |
| | | | |
| | | | |
| | | | |
| | | | |
| | | | |

# THE USBORNE HISTORY OF
# THE TWENTIETH CENTURY

## Christina Hopkinson

### Designed by Russell Punter

### Illustrated by Peter Dennis
Additional Illustrations by Mark Franklin and Dan Courtney

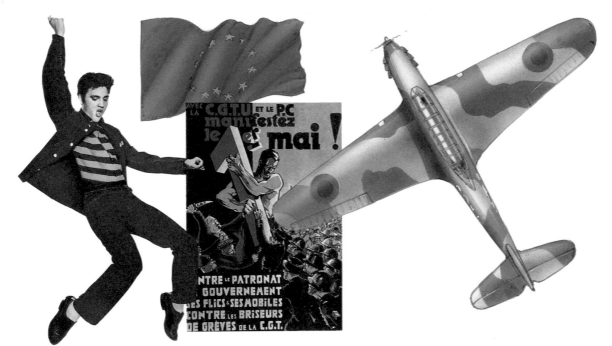

## Edited by Jane Chisholm
### Consultants: Graham Roberts and Peter Wilson
Peter Burnell, Patricia Fara, Martin Kolinsky, Alan Midgley and Richard Tames

With thanks to Milly Trowbridge and Lynn Bresler

# Contents

# Approaching the 20th century

Since 1900, there has been more change, invention and innovation than in any other century. Wars have been fought differently, travel has become quicker and communication easier. In 1900, most Europeans had little idea about how people lived in China. By the 1990s, however, you could fly from Berlin to Beijing in less than a day, and see television pictures of news as it happened.

## THE CENTURY BEFORE

Not all the advances of the century have been new. Many of the ideas and inventions that you will come across in this book actually began in the 19th century, although it was later that they became popular. Communism, a political theory which dominated half of Europe and all of China for most of the 20th century, was first outlined in 1848 by Karl Marx and Friedrich Engels. The record-player, the light bulb, the telephone, X-rays and radio waves were all invented by people in the 19th century. It was also in this era that people began to travel right across the globe and communicate with distant places.

*Signs of the times: Karl Marx, an early X-ray photograph, an early light bulb and an advertisement for a telephone*

## PREDICTIONS

At the start of the century, many scientists, writers and inventors tried to guess what the new century would bring, with varying degrees of success. Most people foresaw improved forms of air travel, but while space exploration was dreamed of, few really believed it could be achieved.

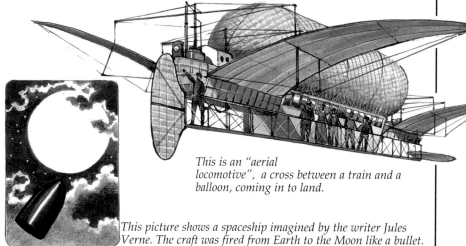

*This is an "aerial locomotive", a cross between a train and a balloon, coming in to land.*

*This picture shows a spaceship imagined by the writer Jules Verne. The craft was fired from Earth to the Moon like a bullet.*

Some predictions proved very accurate. Many believed that women and the people of America and Asia would have greater importance in world affairs. Moving pictures in your own home, and automatic everything were predicted for an age which would see enormous political and technological changes.

*These 19th century cartoons foresee full automation in schools, and air tennis in the year 2000.*

## ABOUT THIS BOOK

Although this book begins with 1900 and finishes with the end of the century, it does not take a year by year approach. Instead it covers the main historical events, such as the First and Second World Wars, and looks at what went on over a longer period in particular parts of the world. The book also picks out technological and cultural changes that span the whole century.

The glossary on pages 80-1 explains the meanings of many words, phrases and terms that appear in this book and might be unfamiliar to you.

Chinese words and names are written with the *pin-yin* system of spelling, which more accurately reproduces the sound of the language. Where the *pin-yin* spelling is less usual, the alternative is given in brackets, for example Beijing (Peking).

# The world in 1900

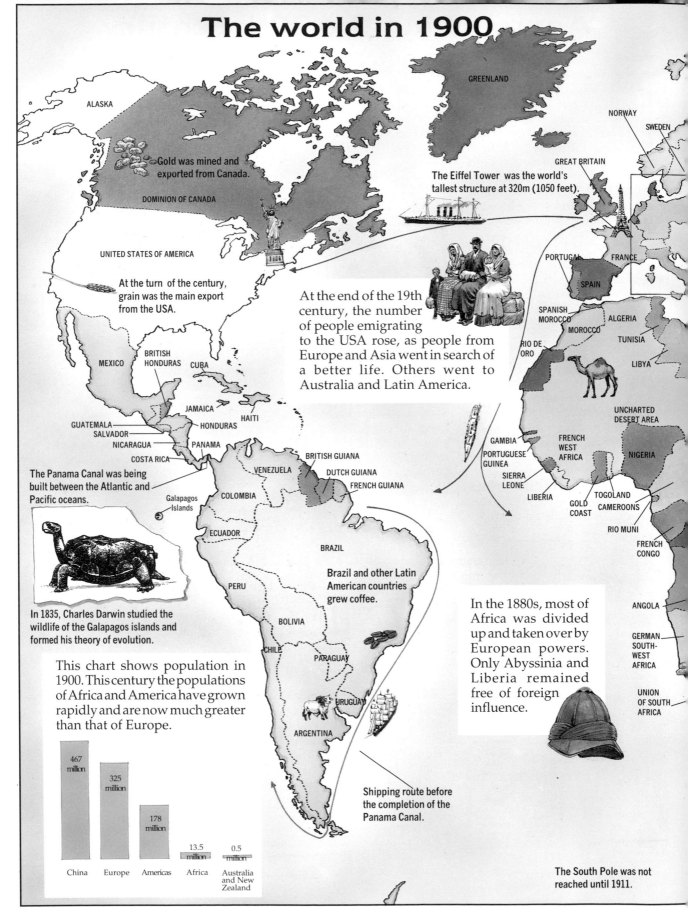

GREENLAND

ALASKA

NORWAY

SWEDEN

GREAT BRITAIN

Gold was mined and exported from Canada.

The Eiffel Tower was the world's tallest structure at 320m (1050 feet).

DOMINION OF CANADA

PORTUGAL

FRANCE

UNITED STATES OF AMERICA

SPAIN

At the turn of the century, grain was the main export from the USA.

At the end of the 19th century, the number of people emigrating to the USA rose, as people from Europe and Asia went in search of a better life. Others went to Australia and Latin America.

SPANISH MOROCCO

ALGERIA

MOROCCO

TUNISIA

RIO DE ORO

LIBYA

MEXICO

BRITISH HONDURAS

CUBA

JAMAICA

HAITI

UNCHARTED DESERT AREA

GUATEMALA

HONDURAS

SALVADOR

NICARAGUA

PANAMA

COSTA RICA

GAMBIA

PORTUGUESE GUINEA

FRENCH WEST AFRICA

NIGERIA

BRITISH GUIANA

VENEZUELA

DUTCH GUIANA

FRENCH GUIANA

SIERRA LEONE

The Panama Canal was being built between the Atlantic and Pacific oceans.

Galapagos Islands

COLOMBIA

LIBERIA

GOLD COAST

TOGOLAND

CAMEROONS

RIO MUNI

ECUADOR

FRENCH CONGO

BRAZIL

In 1835, Charles Darwin studied the wildlife of the Galapagos islands and formed his theory of evolution.

PERU

Brazil and other Latin American countries grew coffee.

ANGOLA

In the 1880s, most of Africa was divided up and taken over by European powers. Only Abyssinia and Liberia remained free of foreign influence.

BOLIVIA

GERMAN SOUTH-WEST AFRICA

CHILE

PARAGUAY

UNION OF SOUTH AFRICA

This chart shows population in 1900. This century the populations of Africa and America have grown rapidly and are now much greater than that of Europe.

URUGUAY

ARGENTINA

Shipping route before the completion of the Panama Canal.

| | | | | |
|---|---|---|---|---|
| 467 million | 325 million | 178 million | 13.5 million | 0.5 million |
| China | Europe | Americas | Africa | Australia and New Zealand |

The South Pole was not reached until 1911.

**Colonial empires**
- Russia
- USA
- Japan
- Britain
- France
- Denmark
- Netherlands
- Belgium
- Italy
- Portugal
- Germany
- Spain
- Semi-colonial
- Independent

DENMARK
NETHERLANDS
GERMANY
BELGIUM LUX
AUSTRIA-HUNGARY
ROMANIA
ITALY
SERBIA
MONTENEGRO
BULGARIA
ALBANIA
GREECE
SWITZERLAND

The Trans-Siberian railway, from China to western Russia, had been mostly built by 1900.

RUSSIAN EMPIRE

KOREA

JAPAN

Chinese fought Europeans in the 1900 Boxer Rebellion.

There were European ports set up along the Chinese coast.

OTTOMAN EMPIRE
Suez Canal
AFGHANISTAN
NEPAL
PERSIA
KUWAIT
EGYPT
CHINESE EMPIRE
BHUTAN
ARABIA
INDIA
BURMA
OMAN
FORMOSA
ADEN
PHILIPPINES
ANGLO-EGYPTIAN SUDAN
ERITREA
GOA
SIAM
FRENCH SOMALILAND
CEYLON
FRENCH INDO-CHINA
BELGIAN CONGO
ABYSSINIA
BRITISH SOMALILAND
UGANDA
ITALIAN SOMALILAND
BRITISH BORNEO
INDIAN OCEAN
MALAYA
BRITISH EAST AFRICA
GERMAN EAST AFRICA
NORTHERN RHODESIA
PORTUGUESE EAST AFRICA
MADAGASCAR
SOUTHERN RHODESIA
BECHUANALAND
SWAZILAND
BASUTOLAND

Malayan rubber was exported for use in bicycle and early car wheels.

Colonialists traded in African elephant tusks.

Tea was the main export from Ceylon.

In 19th century, Britain was unrivalled as the most powerful country in the world. The British Empire was the largest that had ever existed and covered a third of the world's surface. By 1900, this position was threatened by the USA and Germany.

GERMAN NEW GUINEA

DUTCH EAST INDIES

TIMOR

PAPUA

PACIFIC OCEAN

AUSTRALIA

Many went to Australia in search of gold.

The Boer War was being fought between Dutch and British settlers in South Africa. It ended in a British victory in 1902.

The first Zeppelin, a rigid airship filled with gas, flew in 1900.

TASMANIA

NEW ZEALAND

Southern Africa was prized by colonialists for its gold and diamond mines.

New Zealand was the only country where women could vote in elections. Australian women got the vote in 1902.

At the start of the century, the political atmosphere in Europe was tense. The most important countries (known as the Great Powers) were divided by a complicated system of alliances and rivalries, which made the risk of war all the more likely. The strongest partnership was between Germany and the Austro-Hungarian empire (the Central Powers). There was a looser alliance, the Entente, between Britain, France and Russia.

In the 19th century, most of Africa, Asia and the Middle East had been colonized by European countries looking for new areas for investment and for a way of increasing their own prestige. Africa was the main target for these ambitions. By 1900, only 10% of the continent was still free from foreign rule.

Germany, which had only been united as a single country in 1871, was a latecomer to the race to colonize. But the German emperor, Kaiser Wilhelm II, wanted to build an empire to rival those of the French and British. Competition

*Kaiser Wilhelm II*

abroad only increased all the tensions within Europe.

In March 1905, the Kaiser visited Morocco and offered to help the ruling sultan in his struggle to rid the country of French interference. In the conference following the Kaiser's visit, only Austria supported Germany, while the other European powers rejected all German claims for power in North Africa. In 1911, tensions flared up again when the Germans sent a powerful gunboat to the Moroccan port of Agadir, as a protest against the expansion of French power in the area.

## THE ARMS RACE

In the period up to 1914, the Great Powers expanded their armed and naval forces in what was described as an "arms race". Britain felt threatened by German naval expansion. Both countries tried to outdo each other, by building bigger and better battleships. As more and more money was spent on improving war technology, war became increasingly likely.

## BALKAN TROUBLES

The Balkans was Europe's main trouble spot - just as it is today.

*This map shows the troubled Balkan area.*

The region was ruled by Turkey, but many different groups were competing for power. The Slavs in Serbia wanted to dominate all the Slavic areas, while other Balkan states were pressing for independence. Russia and Austria-Hungary also hoped to increase

*In 1906, Britain introduced the first dreadnought, the most powerful ship in the world. Its production speeded up the arms race.*

Ship's kitchen

Officer's cabin

Food stores

Extra provision room

30 cm (12 inch) guns, the biggest yet mounted on a battleship

Funnel for moving the bombshells for firing

Ammunitions store room

Admiral's sea cabin

Shell handling room

*The German gun, Big Bertha*

Firing range of about 14km (9 miles)

Big Bertha weighed as much as a dozen elephants

their power by grabbing land in the area. Austria annexed Bosnia and Herzegovina in 1908.

The First Balkan War broke out in 1912. Serbia, Bulgaria, Greece and Montenegro, formed the Balkan League and attacked Turkey. Turkish troops were driven from Europe within a month. Arguments about the peace treaties led to a Second Balkan War between Bulgaria and the rest of the League. Bulgaria was defeated and Romania, Serbia and Greece all gained territory.

## MURDER AT SARAJEVO

Against this background, it only took a single incident to spark off a major war. On June 28, 1914, at Sarajevo, Bosnia, Archduke Franz Ferdinand, heir to the Austrian throne, was shot and killed by a Serbian nationalist. On July 23, Austria, with German support, demanded that Serbia suppress anti-Austrian groups and dismiss any officials that were not approved by the Austrian government. These were requests that Serbia could not accept if it wanted to remain independent. So the Serbs refused and Austria declared war on July 28.

Russia, in support of Serbia, immediately mobilized its troops on its southern border with Austria.

*Archduke Ferdinand and his wife, shortly before the assassination*

## COUNTDOWN TO WAR

Throughout 1914, the German government had been preparing for battle. They knew that , if war broke out their troops would have to fight on two fronts; against the Russians in the east, and the French in the west. General Schlieffen drew up a plan by which France could be quickly defeated, leaving all the German forces available to fight in the east. Confident that the plan would work, Germany declared war on France on August 3. German troops marched through Belgium to attack France. The British, who had guaranteed Belgium neutrality in 1839, declared war on Germany.

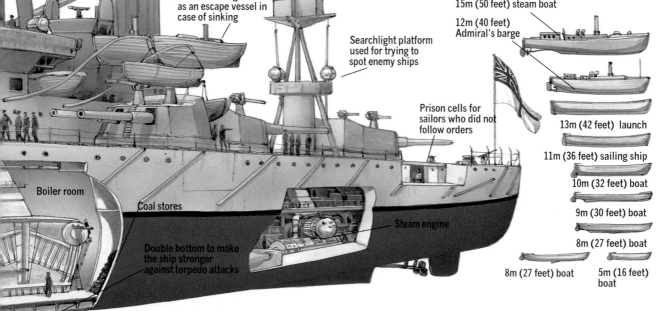

Admiral's barge used as an escape vessel in case of sinking

Searchlight platform used for trying to spot enemy ships

Prison cells for sailors who did not follow orders

Boiler room

Coal stores

Steam engine

Double bottom to make the ship stronger against torpedo attacks

15m (50 feet) steam boat

12m (40 feet) Admiral's barge

13m (42 feet) launch

11m (36 feet) sailing ship

10m (32 feet) boat

9m (30 feet) boat

8m (27 feet) boat

8m (27 feet) boat

5m (16 feet) boat

# The First World War

The war that broke out in August 1914 was really a European war about European issues. But it became known as a "world war" because so many countries outside Europe became directly involved. At first, people believed the war would be short and glorious, but it dragged on for four years, killing 17 million people - many more than in any other conflict in history.

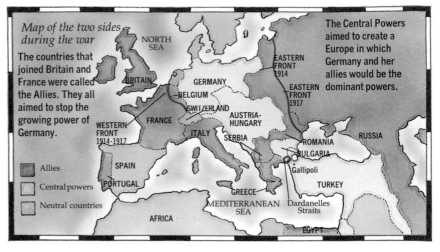

*Map of the two sides during the war*

The countries that joined Britain and France were called the Allies. They all aimed to stop the growing power of Germany.

The Central Powers aimed to create a Europe in which Germany and her allies would be the dominant powers.

- Allies
- Central powers
- Neutral countries

NORTH SEA · BRITAIN · GERMANY · BELGIUM · SWITZERLAND · FRANCE · WESTERN FRONT 1914-1917 · ITALY · AUSTRIA-HUNGARY · SERBIA · EASTERN FRONT 1914 · EASTERN FRONT 1917 · ROMANIA · BULGARIA · RUSSIA · Gallipoli · TURKEY · SPAIN · PORTUGAL · GREECE · MEDITERRANEAN SEA · Dardanelles Straits · AFRICA · EGYPT

## THE SCHLIEFFEN PLAN

The Schlieffen plan assumed that France would be defeated before the Russian forces were ready to fight. But Russia mobilized in only three weeks and invaded Germany and Austria-Hungary. German troops therefore had to fight on both the Western and Eastern fronts.

## TRENCH WARFARE

At the Battle of the Marne in Autumn 1914, the Allies stopped the Germans from advancing deeper into France. Neither side could move forward. To defend themselves, they dug wide parallel ditches called trenches.

From 1915, neither army progressed, and there was a stalemate on both fronts. German troops now occupied Belgian and French territory near the Western front. The Allies tried to expel them from these areas by attacking their trenches. These Allied attacks led to battles in which many thousands of men were killed, but very little land was gained. Successful attacks were almost impossible, because the trenches were so effectively defended by machine guns and barbed wire. At the Battle of the Somme in 1916, 20,000 British troops were killed on the first day alone.

*The troops lived, planned and recovered in these muddy, rat-infested trenches.*

## THE COURSE OF WAR

The Allies tried to break the stalemate on the Western front by securing decisive victories elsewhere. In April 1915, they were joined by Italy. Following a series of unsuccessful attacks, Italy was defeated by Austria-Hungary at Caporetto in 1917. The Italian armies then had to be rescued by French and British troops.

Russia had suffered defeats since the beginning of the war. Very little food or supplies reached the troops on the Eastern front and morale was low. This encouraged support for the communists and helped bring about the Russian Revolution. In March 1918, Lenin, the Bolshevik leader, made peace with the Central Powers at the Treaty of Brest-Litovsk. This strengthened the position of the Germans, who were now free to move their forces to the Western front.

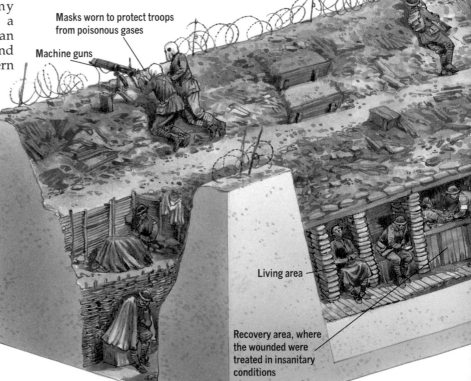

Masks worn to protect troops from poisonous gases

Machine guns

Living area

Recovery area, where the wounded were treated in insanitary conditions

# WAR TECHNOLOGY

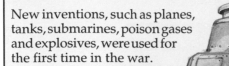

New inventions, such as planes, tanks, submarines, poison gases and explosives, were used for the first time in the war.

*This is an Allied tank, used to break through German trenches in 1918.*

*Aircraft, like this one flown by Von Richthofen ("the Red Baron"), flew over enemy lines to obtain information.*

## MEDITERRANEAN WAR

From 1915, the Allies tried to divert forces away from the Western front by attacking in the east. Allied naval forces were sent to the Dardanelles Straits and Gallipoli in Turkey and to Salonika in Greece.

Thousands of troops were killed, many of them from New Zealand and Australia. By 1918, the Allies controlled parts of Iran and Iraq and most of Syria and Palestine.

*A North African soldier*

Barbed wire to defend the trench

Rats fed on the food and flesh of the trench.

## WAR ON THE WAVES

In autumn 1914, all the German ships outside the North Sea were destroyed in a series of naval actions by British forces. As a result, Germany was left unable to defend her African and Pacific colonies.

The Allies used their naval supremacy to search German ships in the North Sea and to confiscate their goods on board. By the winter of 1916, Germany was suffering from severe shortages of raw materials and food.

From 1915, the Germans reacted to these raids by using submarines, called U-boats, to sink British ships on sight. Many of these ships were carrying imported food from British colonies. As a result, shortages became serious in Britain too.

## US INTERVENTION

In 1915, a German U-boat sank an British passenger liner called the *Lusitania*, with the loss of 1,198 lives. The Germans believed that the ship was carrying Allied weapons. Provoked by continued German submarine attacks on ships, the USA declared war on Germany in April 1917. Until the U-boat campaign, the US govern-ment had firmly stated that it would not join the war.

*The sinking of the Lusitania*

## THE END OF THE WAR

By 1918, the Central Powers were losing the war. All the countries involved were exhausted, but the Allies easily outnumbered their enemies, having been joined by 18 other states in the course of the war. The German leaders realized that they would have to act very quickly in order to defeat the Allies, who were now supported by fresh US forces. On the Western front, German generals then launched a last series of major attacks, known as the Ludendorff Offensive.

*German and Allied leaders signing the armistice ending the war*

After some initial success, the Germans were forced to retreat. Their troops were no match for the larger Allied forces, with their extensive and effective use of tanks.

Meanwhile, Turkey was defeated by British forces in the Middle East and Austria-Hungary was defeated in Italy. Faced with military defeat and the threat of revolution at home, the Germans surrendered on November 11, bringing an end to four years of war.

# The aftermath of war

The First World War is often described as the first "total war" because of its dramatic effects. During the four years of fighting, new weapons were used, empires fell, vast areas suffered terrible damage and millions were killed. The Allies met in Paris in 1919 to decide on a peace settlement.

## THE BIG THREE

The peace treaties were mainly the result of negotiations between the US president, Woodrow Wilson, the British prime minister, David Lloyd George, and the French premier, Georges Clemenceau. Together they were known as "the big three", but each wanted something different from the settlement. In January 1918, Wilson set out his principles in 14 points. His main aims were to reform the way nations dealt with each other, to reduce weapon reserves and to create ways in which wars could be prevented. Clemenceau wanted French military superiority in Europe and revenge on Germany. Lloyd George was also under pressure from the British people to impose harsh terms on Germany.

*Lloyd George, Clemenceau and Wilson*

The eventual settlement consisted of several treaties. The Treaty of Versailles was concerned with Germany. In Article 231, known as "the war guilt clause", the Germans were forced to accept blame for the war, and had to pay reparations, in the form of large sums of money, to the victorious nations. Germany also had to reduce its fighting capacity. It was prohibited from having an airforce or submarines, and allowed only six battleships.

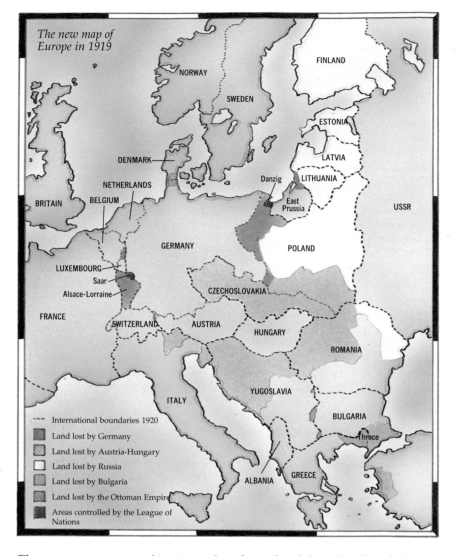

*The new map of Europe in 1919*

- - - International boundaries 1920
- Land lost by Germany
- Land lost by Austria-Hungary
- Land lost by Russia
- Land lost by Bulgaria
- Land lost by the Ottoman Empire
- Areas controlled by the League of Nations

The army was restricted in size and troops were banned from the Rhine area, close to France. Germany's overseas colonies in Africa and the Far East were divided among the Allies. German territory in Europe was also lost. The rich industrial provinces of Alsace and Lorraine (seized by Germany in 1871) were retaken by France.

By the treaties of St. Germain and Trianon, Austria and Hungary were separated from each other, and their territory was reduced.

Smaller countries were created

*German tanks were destroyed as part of the settlement.*

from land lost by the defeated states. Poland expanded by absorbing territory lost by Germany and Russia. The republic of Czechoslovakia was established, containing Czechs and Slovaks, as well as Polish, Hungarian and German minorities. A large multi-racial Balkan state, Yugoslavia, was formed by uniting Serbia, Slovenia, Croatia, Bosnia and Montenegro. Latvia, Lithuania, Estonia and Finland, former provinces of the Russian empire, became independent.

## LEAGUE OF NATIONS

The last of Wilson's 14 points proposed the formation of a League of Nations, an organization of countries to enforce international law, prevent future wars and secure the independence of all nations. But the US Senate wanted America to isolate itself from European affairs, and refused to allow the USA to join the League. Without US economic and military power, the League was weak. During the 1920s and 1930s, 42 nations met in annual assemblies, but the League was unable to enforce its will over aggressive countries (see pages 24-5).

## POLITICAL EFFECTS

Many people were unhappy with the post-war settlements. Germans resented the war-guilt clause, while those in victorious countries, such as Italy and Japan, did not think they had been properly rewarded. Ruling monarchies crumbled after defeat. In 1918, German socialists overthrew the Hohenzollern king. The Turkish and Austrian monarchies were replaced with republics. Democratic governments were set up in countries with no tradition of democracy and often proved unable to rule effectively. In this climate, extreme political theories, such as communism and fascism, became popular. The new borders were not respected and this led to local battles.

The victorious powers were also weakened by the war. Britain found that it could no longer maintain its huge empire. In Ireland, part of Britain since 1801, opposition to British rule escalated. In 1921, the southern part of the country was made a self-governing colony, or dominion.

*Mustapha Kemal, the leader of the new Turkish Republic*

## SOCIAL CHANGES

In the immediate years after the war, the inhabitants of Belgium, Germany and Austria suffered from a terrible lack of food. As a result, many people died of starvation. All over Europe, millions also died in a massive influenza ('flu) epidemic in 1919.

A more lasting effect of the war was financial insecurity in Europe. The war had been paid for with huge loans, and some governments printed more and more money to pay off these debts. This resulted in inflation, as printed money came to be worth less and less, and goods became more expensive. Governments had to concentrate on paying off debts and rebuilding economies. This meant that they had little left to spend on social benefits for returning soldiers, the unemployed, and families who had suffered losses.

*Ex-soldiers working as street-peddlars*

With so many men away at the front, women had become more involved in working in places outside the home. Some continued to work in factories and on farms after the war, where they were shown to be at least as capable and hardworking as men. In many places this helped to break down resistance to the idea of women being involved in politics, industry and working life. In Germany, Britain and the USA, women gained the right to vote in elections soon after the war. But in other places, such as Italy and France, they had to wait a lot longer to get the vote (see page 75).

A. F. L.
VOTES FOR WOMEN.

*A women's rights protestor and a British women's rights emblem*

During the war, it had been essential for governments to maintain good relations with workers. Any industrial unrest would have damaged the country's ability to provide supplies for the war front. As a result, workers' groups, called trade unions, grew in strength and this continued after the war. In 1926, British unions led a six day general strike, when people from many trades refused to work. Although their demands were refused by the government, their action plunged the country into a state of national emergency.

*During the strike, workers tried to stop transport by blocking the roads.*

*This cartoon by Will Dyson in 1919 predicts that the problems left by the war will lead to another conflict.*

# The Russian Revolution

The coronation of Tsar Nicholas II in 1894 was attended by so many that a thousand subjects were crushed to death. The Russian empire, over a sixth of the world's land, was one of the most backward in Europe. All decisions were made by the tsar and put into action by a lumbering system of clerks. Russia even followed the Julian calendar, which was 13 days behind the Gregorian one, used by most of Europe since 1582.

*The tsar's crown jewels*

## 1905 REVOLUTION

In 1904, the tsarist government tried to increase its popularity by waging a glorious war against Japan. But instead, its position was made worse by a series of terrible defeats. Anger about the war and poor living conditions sparked off political demands by the workers. In January 1905, a peaceful group marched to the Winter Palace in St. Petersburg to ask for changes in the running of the empire. Troops fired into the crowd without warning, killing many people. This incident was known as Bloody Sunday and led to riots among the people, and in the army and navy.

*Russian workers barricaded the streets of Moscow during the 1905 revolution.*

The pressure for change, which came from peasants, workers and middle class liberals, led to a promise from the tsar that he would set up an elected advisory council, called a *duma*.

## REFORM AND FAILURE

After 1905, Peter Stolypin, a government minister, tried to modernize Russia's economy. He wanted to make land available for the peasants to own privately by lending them state money. It was hoped that this measure would create a class of wealthy, efficient peasants called *kulaks*.

But the political reforms did not last. The first and second dumas were closed down within weeks of opening for criticizing the tsar. The third was more submissive and survived until 1917.

## GROWING OPPOSITION

In the first two decades of the century, radical solutions were put forward to the problems of tsarist rule. The Russian Social Democratic and Labour Party, formed in 1898, had some members who held communist ideas. In 1903, the party split into two groups: Bolsheviks and Mensheviks. The Bolsheviks were led by a dynamic young lawyer named Vladimir Ilyich Ulyanov, later known as Lenin. He was repeatedly imprisoned and exiled by the state, but kept returning to Russia in the hope of inspiring a revolution.

*Vladimir Lenin*

## THE FIRST WORLD WAR

In 1914, Russia declared war on Austria and Germany. By the summer of 1915, the war was going very badly for the Russian forces. To try to reverse this, the tsar took command of the army in person, although he had no experience of military matters. Government policy was left in the hands of his unpopular German wife, Tsarina Alexandra, whose advisors were either incompetent or corrupt. The most famous was Rasputin, a monk who was said to hold a frightening power over Alexandra.

*Cartoon showing Rasputin in the middle of the royal household*

## FEBRUARY REVOLUTION

Russia's economy was not prepared for war, and there were great food shortages. In St. Petersburg protests broke out in February 1917, and carried on for five days. In the factories, strike committees and workers' councils, called Soviets, were formed. The tsar saw that his position was impossible and so resigned his throne, ending 300 years of rule by his family. Senior men from the duma set up the Provisional Government, based in the Winter Palace.

*The Litovosky prison was set on fire as a protest.*

## OCTOBER REVOLUTION

German politicians wanted to encourage political disorder in Russia, as they believed it would remove the country from the war. In April 1917, they helped Lenin to return to Russia in a protected train carriage from exile in Switzerland.

On the night of October 24, Lenin and his followers stormed the Winter Palace. There was little bloodshed because there was little resistance. On October 26, the All Russian Congress of Soviets accepted the take over by the Bolsheviks. The "revolution" was in fact a well-planned seizure of power, organized and carried out by a few.

*The Bolsheviks fired cannon from the battleship Aurora.*

## DEATH OF THE TSAR

After giving up the throne, Tsar Nicholas, his wife and their five children were exiled to distant parts of the empire. In July 1918, they were shot and killed by Soviet guards. Before the discovery of the bodies in 1992, there were claims that not all the children were dead.

*The Tsar and his family shortly before their deaths*

## THE CIVIL WAR

Map showing the areas of influence during the Civil War
- ☐ Counter-revolutionary "white" army territory
- ■ Territory controlled by the Soviets

St. Petersburg

RUSSIA

## BOLSHEVIKS IN POWER

In the elections for a new government, only a quarter of the voters chose the Bolsheviks. The party was popular in the cities, but not in the villages. The Bolsheviks maintained control by launching the "Red Terror", a campaign of arrests and executions.

In March 1918, Russia withdrew from the war, losing huge amounts of territory from its old empire in the Treaty of Brest-Litovsk.

*Memories of old Russia, like this statue of Tsar Alexander III, were removed.*

Between 1918 and 1920, there was a civil war, between the Bolsheviks and those against the revolution, and also between Russians and non-Russians in the old empire. The Bolshevik forces were called the Red Army, while their enemies were known as Whites. Although the Whites had foreign aid, the Soviet Red Army won because it was better organized and led.

*Both sides used propaganda. The Red poster, above, asks "Have you joined the Red Army?". The second shows a White view of communists.*

## BIRTH OF THE SOVIET UNION

Even after the civil war, things were not secure for the Soviets. Food was not reaching the cities and industrial production was a quarter of its 1913 level. In 1920-21, there was a terrible famine in parts of the nation. To try to solve these problems, the New Economic Policy was introduced, allowing a limited return to capitalism.

In December 1922, having crushed all opposition, Russia, along with most of the lands of the old tsarist empire was renamed the Union of Socialist Soviet Republics (USSR). It was known by this name for 69 years.

*The hammer and sickle, representing workers of factory and field, was the emblem of the USSR.*

# The growth of the USA

In the first three decades of the 20th century, the United States of America established itself as the most powerful nation in the world. It experienced a huge growth in population, industry and wealth, and was recognized as an important naval power. But this boom was not without its problems, many of which became apparent in 1929, with the collapse of the US stock market (see page 18). The expanding nation was also troubled by poverty, crime and racism.

## A NEW WORLD

Between 1900 and 1920, over 14 million Europeans emigrated to America. These people, often poor and oppressed, came because they believed that they could find a better life. In the 19th century, the immigrants had been mainly from Britain, Germany and Ireland, but the new wave was from southern and eastern Europe: Poland, Italy, Austria and Russia. Many came to escape the political upheavals and persecutions of their native countries; others came to escape poverty. They brought with them new languages, traditions and religions into the USA.

*A typical New York street in the 1920s*

## THE KU KLUX KLAN

In the 1910s and 1920s, some white people in the southern states reacted against the arrival of these new immigrants. They joined a secret and powerful group called the Ku Klux Klan which violently attacked blacks, Roman Catholics and Jews. In some areas of the USA, the Klan became so powerful that it took over the law.

*The Ku Klux Klan wore sinister white costumes with masks to hide their identities.*

There were more cinemas in New York than any in other city, although by the 1920s films were being made in Hollywood on the west coast of the USA.

Immigrants arrived at Ellis island, just outside New York, and came to the city with only a few bags.

PARADISE THEATRE

Charlie Chaplin CITY LIGHTS

Cinemas made stars of actors like Charlie Chaplin.

Model T-Ford

## MASS PRODUCTION

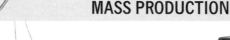

Model T Fords were built on an "assembly line".

The car frame ran along a track.

Each time it stopped, a part was added to it .

At the end of the line, the car was ready to drive.

In 1908, the first production line car, the "Model T" Ford, was introduced in Detroit. Henry Ford, the owner of the company, aimed to build cars much more quickly and cheaply than ever before, so that more people could afford to buy one. In 1909, there were 12,000 cars on the world's roads. By 1929, there were 26 million cars in the USA alone. American cities grew around bigger roads designed for car use.

## BIG CITY LIFE

Immigration and industry led to the growth of cities, so that by 1930 over half the population lived in large towns. Most recent immigrants lived with people of their own race or nationality in poor city districts known as ghettos.

New York City was the symbol of America's growth. During the 1920s, work began on the tallest structure the world had ever seen. The Empire State Building, which opened in 1913, had 102 floors and was 380m (1250 feet) high.

The Empire State Building

Before the end of prohibition, people drank in secret bars behind shops and houses.

Jazz music and dancing was popular at this time.

## THE JAZZ AGE

The 1920s were known as the Jazz Age, because of the new music and dances which became popular. Women wore shorter dresses and shorter hair, and many people did a new dance called the Charleston.

In 1920, the government forbade the drinking of alcohol, but many people drank it secretly in illegal bars called speakeasies. The government believed that there would be less crime if they banned drinks like whisky. In fact, there was more. Criminals, known as gangsters, made a lot of money by making and selling alcohol. People were beaten or killed unless they paid protection money to the gangsters.

## AMERICAN INDUSTRY

By 1910, the USA consumed more oil and natural gas than the rest of the world put together. It produced as much steel as Britain and Germany combined, and was the world's leading producer of copper and cotton.

Industrial and economic growth continued in the 1920s and the dollar became the strongest currency in the world. During the course of the decade, the amount earned by each worker rose from $500 to $700 a year, but all this was to change in 1929, when America's stock market collapsed, and the country was plunged into depression.

## THE USA ABROAD

*This map shows US possessions.*

The US government wanted the country to be as strong abroad as it was at home. In 1898, it gained control of Cuba and Puerto Rico in the Caribbean, and the Philippine islands and Hawaii in the Pacific. The government claimed to be acting to protect these lands from European colonization, but the move also secured better trading relations and international naval bases for the USA.

In 1903, the USA leased land in Panama and started building a 80km (50 mile) canal there to make a waterway between the Pacific and the Atlantic. When the canal finally opened in 1913, it was hailed as the world's greatest engineering feat. Ownership of it gave the USA a great military and economic advantage.

The US government also became very active in Mexico by building railways in its northern territory. This guaranteed US economic and industrial involvement in the country. The Mexican dictator, Porfirio Diaz, wanted to ally with the USA, but he was overthrown in 1911, in a revolution led by Pancho Villa. The revolution was followed by a time of lawlessness and disorder, which threatened the US position in Mexico.

*Mexican revolutionaries wore traditional clothes.*

# 中國 China and Japan 1900-1945 日本

In the 19th and early 20th centuries, colonization and trade increased European and American influence in Asia. China and Japan, the two most important independent empires in the area, reacted to the experience in very different ways.

## CHINA

For thousands of years, the Chinese had thought of themselves as the most important and civilized people in Asia. Instead of imitating the developments of the West, China resisted anything non-Asian. Some modern western ideas were brought in during the 19th century, when France, Russia and Britain founded ports, such as Shanghai, along the Chinese coast. But despite this, China did not change either its industries or its system of ruling.

*The red dragon, the ancient symbol of China*

## THE BOXER REBELLION

In 1900, a secret society called the Harmonious Fists led a rising in protest against the intrusion of European merchants. The revolt became known as the Boxer rebellion, because the protesters believed that a training in Chinese martial arts, including boxing, would protect them from foreign bullets. The uprising was brutally crushed by an international force made up of soldiers from Britain, France, Japan and Russia. These countries divided the wealthy Chinese coastal areas into blocks under their control.

*A Boxer rebel training in martial arts*

## THE LAST EMPEROR

Since 1644, China had been ruled by the Manchu dynasty, which had made little effort to modernize its government. When the Empress Zi Xi (Tzu Hsi) died in 1908, she was replaced by her two year old nephew Pu Yi. Chinese politicians took advantage of his youth to introduce limited democracy. In 1910, a national assembly met for the first time.

*Two year old Pu Yi (right), with his father and brother*

## FALL OF THE MANCHUS

The government's attempts to reform came too late. In 1911, the Manchus were overthrown by a group of revolutionary nationalists, called the Guomindang (Kuomintang), who wanted full democracy. They declared a republic. This was followed by a period of unrest and local rule by warlords, who controlled small armies. Discontent with the Guomindang and divisions in the country led to the foundation of the Chinese Communist Party. In 1925, the commander of the Guomindang army, Jiang Jie shi (Chiang Kai-shek) became leader of the republicans. In 1928, Jiang was declared President of the Republic of China.

## THE LONG MARCH

Jiang's presidency was challenged by the leader of the Communist Party, Mao Zedong (Mao Tse-tung). Mao's aim was to build support in the countryside before spreading communism in the cities. In 1931, he proclaimed a Chinese Soviet Republic in the remote Jiangxi province, but three years later Jiang Jie shi drove the communists away from their stronghold. This forced Mao to lead his 10,000 supporters on a 8000km (5000 mile) walk across China. This dangerous journey is known as the Long March. At the end, they set up a communist government at Yenan, a region in the north-west which is protected by mountains. From his base in Yenan, Mao plotted to take over the whole country (see page 58).

*The Long March of the communists*

Two thirds of the marchers died on the way.

Baggage was carried by horses.

The march included women and children.

Mao Zedong

## JAPAN

Following a period of rapid industrialization, which included the introduction of a railway system and improvements in education, Japan entered the 20th century as the only country in Asia with a western-style economy.

## WAR WITH RUSSIA

In 1904, Japan went to war with Russia over control of Manchuria and Korea. Manchuria, which was rich in resources, was ruled by the Chinese Manchu dynasty, while Korea was independent. The Russian military forces were backward when compared with those of the newly industrialized Japanese. As a result, Japan fought the Russian army to a standstill and completely destroyed their navy. The 1905 Treaty of Portsmouth, which brought the war to an end, gave Japan control over Korea. Manchuria remained part of China, but with Japanese economic domination.

*This Japanese print shows their heroic soldiers defeating the Russians.*

In the First World War, Japan fought with the Allies against the Central Powers. During the war, Japan conquered German colonies in China and the Pacific. The peace conferences that followed the war recognized Japan's status as a world power and gave the country new territory.

## JAPAN IN THE DEPRESSION

Japan was hit very hard by the collapse of world trade in 1929 (see pages 18-19). Many Japanese people believed that a strong army and the annexing of foreign territory was the answer to all their economic problems. In 1931, Japan invaded the nearby state of Manchuria. The following year a dependent puppet state under the rule of Pu Yi (the deposed ex-emperor of China) was quickly established.

*The Japanese emperor's flag*

Although the Japanese emperor was worshipped as a god and was supposed to have unlimited powers, his position grew weaker during the 1930s. The army began to take over the running of the country and economic policies were directed at maintaining military strength.

## JAPAN'S INVASION OF CHINA

*This map shows Japan's progress into China.*

CHINA

Beijing

JAPAN

PACIFIC OCEAN

Yenan

Shanghai

Hankow

Canton

Hong Kong

Area occupied by Japan in 1944

Area occupied by Japan in 1938

Route of the Long March.

In 1937, Japan invaded China and conquered its coastal areas. Although the Japanese failed to gain control of the whole country, the Chinese forces were unable to expel the Japanese troops. Japan became involved in the Second World War when Japanese leaders signed a pact with Germany in 1936. In December 1941, the Japanese air force unexpectedly attacked the US Pacific naval base at Pearl Harbor. This act resulted in a declaration of war on Japan by the USA and Britain. By the following year, the Japanese had occupied much of Southeast Asia and the Pacific. In February 1942, they captured the main British base at Singapore. Later that year they united many of the countries in the area under Japanese control in an economic and political pact.

At first, the bombing of Pearl Harbor weakened the US position, as many of their ships were destroyed. Later, their superior forces led to a series of US victories. But despite heavy losses, the Japanese people did not surrender until August 1945, when the Allies dropped two atomic bombs and the USSR declared war.

*Japanese soldiers in Beijing*

# The Great Depression

From 1929 to the mid-1930s, much of the world was plunged into an economic slump, which brought enormous poverty and unemployment, and sent wages and production levels crashing. This is known as the Great Depression.

*Many returning soldiers, often injured, were forced to beg to survive.*

## WARNING SIGNS

The first signs that depression was on the way came after the First World War. The cost of weapons and armies had left many countries with huge debts. The introduction of new technology increased food production in Europe, Australia and America, but the demand for food stayed the same. This led to falling food prices, and forced many farmers out of business.

An international economic crisis was also made more likely by an imbalance in world trade. The problem was that the USA was exporting more goods than it was importing. The countries that bought US goods often borrowed from US banks to pay for them.

This meant that any collapse in the US economy would be felt all over the world. Germany had the biggest debts to US banks, because of money borrowed to meet the reparation payments to the Allies.

Another reason for the imbalance was that the old industrial countries such as Britain and France were producing goods made from steel and cotton, which other countries no longer bought in the same quantities. Electrical goods, chemicals and cars had replaced them as the most popular imports.

In 1925, the situation was made worse by the decision in Britain to return to the Gold Standard. This was a rate of exchange based on the amount of gold that each country had in reserve, but it was calculated on 19th century estimates that were no longer accurate. The Gold Standard made European currencies strong in relation to the American dollar, and this made their goods very expensive abroad.

*In the 1920s, people wanted US electrical goods, like this vacuum cleaner.*

## WALL STREET CRASH

Although the Depression had long-term causes, what triggered it was the collapse of the New York Stock Market, on Wall Street, in October 1929. During the 1920s, there had been rapid growth in the USA. It became popular for ordinary Americans to speculate on the stock

*The New York Stock Exchange on Wall Street*

exchange by buying and selling shares in businesses. The more shares were traded, the higher their price rose, until shares became over-valued. Many people built up large debts by borrowing from banks to buy more shares.

*The losses after the Crash led some to turn from stockbroking to car dealing.*

By 1929, many people began to believe that their shares were not worth as much as they had paid for them. So they began to sell them off quickly. Shareholders panicked and rushed to get rid of stock. Prices plummeted, and on October 24, 13 million shares changed hands. Within a week, American investors had lost over $40 million. This is known as the Wall Street Crash. The US economy went from boom to slump in only a few months. Thousands rushed to cash in all their savings, in what is known as a "run" on the banks. But the banks did not have the money to give their account holders. Over 9000 banks were forced to close and many people lost their entire savings.

*This cartoon symbolizes the Wall Street market crashing.*

In the worst years of the Depression, from 1929 to 1933, agricultural prices fell by almost two-thirds, industrial production halved, businesses went bankrupt, and millions lost their jobs.

As many people had lost their jobs, soup kitchens selling cheap food became very popular.

LINE FOR
1¢ RESTAURANT
20 MEALS 1¢
DONATIONS WANTED
HELP FEED THE HUNGRY
I WILL FEED 20
1¢ RESTAURANT
107 W 43ᵈ ST

## WORLD DEPRESSION

The Depression was not limited to the USA. It affected almost every economy in the world. Australia, Austria, Poland, Canada, Latin America and the Netherlands were all severely hit. The country with the biggest debts was Germany, which had already suffered a crash in 1923 (see page 22-23).

*This picture shows poor people living in old drainpipes in Tokyo, Japan.*

In 1931, Germany was plunged into another crisis when the Bank of Vienna collapsed. At the peak of the crisis, one in three German workers was unemployed.

Recovery was slow. It took many years for employment to return to old levels. Chile, Japan and Sweden had restored industrial production by 1935, but for most countries the process took much longer.

*In the mid-1930s, a fierce wind blew through the west of the USA, known as the Dustbowl. This farm shows the effects.*

## GOVERNMENT RESPONSE

At first, government responses to the Depression were ineffective. Each country tried to protect its own economy by demanding high duties on imported goods. This weakened world trade. Governments tried to work together at the World Economic Conference held in 1933, but no practical decisions were made.

In 1932, Franklin D. Roosevelt was elected US President. He introduced a series of policies, known as the New Deal, to help kick-start the country out of depression. The New Deal included projects to build roads and electricity stations.

Kick out DEPRESSION WITH A DEMOCRATIC VOTE

NRA MEMBER U.S. WE DO OUR PART

*A National Recovery Administration badge*

*US Democratic Party slogan*

## THE PEOPLE'S RESPONSE

In this atmosphere of economic uncertainty, many people were attracted to extremist political groups, such as fascists and communists, which offered radical solutions. In Germany, Adolf Hitler was elected because he offered a simple solution to unemployment and poverty. Many Germans thought that, unless they voted for him, the communists would come to power. Fascist groups also gained support in Austria, the Balkans, Spain, South America and Britain. In France, a communist-socialist government came to power in 1936.

*An Italian poster for a fascist festival*

VEGLIONE TRICOLORE
PRO LEGIONARI FASCISTI

TEATRO LIRICO
V = III = MCMXX

AVEC LA C.G.T.U ET LE P.C manifestez le 1er mai !
CONTRE LE PATRONAT LE GOUVERNEMENT SES FLICS ET SES MOBILES CONTRE LES BRISEURS DE GRÈVES DE LA C.G.T.

*A poster produced by a communist led union in France*

An alternative to these was offered by the British economist John Maynard Keynes. He argued that governments should take a greater role in economic affairs, without strictly controlling it. Poorer people should be protected from poverty by better health care, education and unemployment benefits.

*Hunger marches were a popular way of demanding change.*

FIGHTING FOR BREAD AND TURNS

# Stalin's USSR

Josef Stalin, the man who succeeded Lenin as leader of the Soviet Union, had a reputation for being tough, ruthless and determined. His early career involved a good deal of illegal activity, including bank robbery. Stalin came from Georgia, a province of the Russian empire, and changed his name, Djugashvili, to Stalin, meaning "man of steel". Lenin had severely criticized him in a document written during the long illness that led to his death in 1924. But Stalin had suppressed the document and was always careful to associate himself with the great founder of the revolution.

*The Kremlin and Red Square in Moscow*

GUM, the state department store

Main arcade of GUM

Every year, there were huge military parades to celebrate the 1917 revolution.

In the USSR this area was known as Ploshchad Revolutsii (Revolution Square).

*Map of the USSR*

RUSSIA

Leningrad

Moscow

UKRAINE

BLACK SEA

GEORGIA

## STRUGGLE FOR POWER

Stalin's main rivals for power were Trotsky, the leader of the Red Army, and two senior members of the Communist Party, Kamenev and Zinoviev. Trotsky believed that the goal of the party should be to spread revolution across the world, a policy called internationalism. Stalin argued that the revolution should be secured in Russia first. At the Communist Party's 14th Party Congress, the delegates rejected internationalism in support of Stalin's "socialism in one country". This enabled Stalin to take control of government appointments. By 1927, Zinoviev, Trotsky, Kamenev and their allies had been thrown out of the party. Trotsky was exiled to live abroad, where he continued to criticize Stalin. In 1940, he was murdered with an ice pick by a Stalinist agent.

## ECONOMIC REVOLUTION

Stalin pushed the USSR to industrialize, in order for it to compete with the rest of the world. In December 1927, the 15th Communist Party Congress agreed that the state planning agency (the section in charge of production) should be given greater powers. The agency drew up the first Five Year Plan, outlining production targets to be reached by 1933. New coal and iron mines and industrial complexes were opened throughout the USSR.

To pay for these changes in industry, the peasants were

УДАРНУЮ УБОРКУ—

БОЛЬШЕВИСТСКОМУ УРОЖАЮ

*This poster makes the life of the peasant seem heroic.*

required to produce more grain to sell abroad, and to feed the growing number of workers in Soviet cities. Stalin regarded the land-owning peasants known as kulaks as a serious threat to his plans. His solution was to attempt to wipe them out as a class by introducing a radical new policy called collectivization.

From 1929, all agricultural land was merged into large government farms. By 1930, 60 million people had been forced to move to these land blocks, known as *kolkhoz*, or "collective farms".

St. Basil's Cathedral, built in the 16th century

The Cathedral's ornate style contrasts with the plainness of the mausoleum.

Crowds at a military parade

The overall length of the walls is 2235m (680 feet).

Lenin's mausoleum, where he is preserved in an open coffin

The Senate Building, used by communists as the party headquarters

The Sverdlov hall, used for party meetings and ceremonies

Between 1934 and 1937, Stalin accused almost every leading communist of being an enemy of the revolution. Even men such as Zinoviev and Kamenev, who had made the revolution, were tried and put to death. In just two years, Stalin executed a third of all Soviet army officers. Having killed men who had played a part in the revolution, he went on to alter the history

*A poster of Stalin*

books, making himself appear as Lenin's closest ally. The faces of Trotsky and other party leaders accused of crimes were removed from photos and replaced with that of Stalin. In old Bolshevik photos, Stalin hovers beside Lenin, while Trotsky is nowhere to be seen.

President Khrushchev, the party leader from 1953 to 1964, tried to correct some of Stalin's lies. But President Gorbachev was the first to open up Soviet archives fully to historians.

## PROPAGANDA

Stalin relied on newspapers, film and art to promote his policies. He encouraged a style of art known as Soviet Socialist Realism. Despite its name, it was not a realistic portrayal of the life of a peasant or worker, but a glorified picture of communist society.

*This statue shows solidarity between an industrial worker and a collective farm worker.*

Stalin saw any resistance to this as evidence of kulak presence, although in fact it was often the poorer peasants who preferred the old way of farming. Many killed their animals rather than lose them to the *kolkhoz*. This led to a shortage of livestock, and to the arrest of many of the best farmers. In 1932, millions of people died of starvation in the Ukraine, the main grain-producing region, while the state continued to make money by exporting food abroad.

## STALIN'S PURGES

In 1919, Lenin built prison camps called *gulags*, where moderates, conservative army officers and monarchists were imprisoned or executed. Under Stalin, the camps overflowed with intellectuals, writers and kulaks. Even people who simply did not meet the goals of the Five Year Plans might be jailed. More and more camps had to be built in order to hold the growing number of prisoners. It is estimated that Stalin's policies resulted in 15 million deaths.

# The rise of fascism

Between the two world wars, Europe was in the grip of an extremist political ideology known as fascism. Fascist parties swept to power in several countries, using brutality to gain support. The term, first coined by the Italian dictator Mussolini, is used to describe theories based on nationalism and dictatorship.

*Fascism comes from the Latin word "fasces", a bundle of rods symbolizing authority in Ancient Rome.*

## MUSSOLINI'S ITALY

The Italian government was weakened by the First World War, and was unable to deal with the social and economic problems it left behind. Many Italians believed that communism was the solution, while others believed that a revival of the values of the empire of ancient Rome would make Italy great again.

Benito Mussolini (1883-1945) began his political career as a socialist, but became dissatisfied with left-wing ideas and founded his own political party, *Fasci del Combattimento* ("Fascists for the Battle"), in 1919.

*Benito Mussolini*

## THE APPEAL OF FASCISM

Mussolini claimed he would make Italy strong and powerful. Fascism was seen as protection against communism, and so was especially appealing to the two most powerful groups in Italy: the industrialists and the Catholic Church.

## FASCISM IN ACTION

In the early 1920s, fascists fought communists in industrial disputes, and gained popular support. In October 1922, fascists marched to Rome, where they forced the king, Victor Emmanuel III, to make Mussolini prime minister.

Mussolini soon built up a dicatorship. He passed the Acerbo laws, giving his party more seats in parliament, and used violence against his opponents. In 1926, he banned new political parties and declared that parliament was to be made up from a list of candidates drawn up by him.

The fascists controlled all levels of society. Workers and bosses were forced to join unions run by them. A major plan of public works was put into action, in the hope that it would lead to economic recovery.

*The march on Rome in 1922*

## PROBLEMS IN GERMANY

In 1918, a socialist revolution overthrew the German monarchy, setting up a republic, the Weimar Republic, in its place. The new government had to deal with opposition from the army, right-wing nationalists and communists.

Many Germans were angry about the harsh post-war peace settlement and the government could not pay the huge reparations payments. In 1923, there was a general strike in the Ruhr valley, followed by economic collapse and massive inflation.

*Children played with worthless German currency.*

After this collapse, the French and British governments agreed to a more relaxed system of payments. A large US investment plan helped the German economy to recover, but another major setback came in 1929 with the Wall Street Crash.

## HITLER AND THE NAZIS

Adolf Hitler was born in Austria in 1889. After failing to become a professional artist, he became involved in the German Workers Party. This later developed into the extreme right-wing National Socialist German Workers party, known as the Nazis, led by Hitler.

Hitler and his party believed that Germans were superior to the Jews and other races.

*Adolf Hitler*

His aim was to set up a strongly controlled state of "pure" Germans (who he called Aryans), under a powerful leader, or *fuhrer*. This state would be at the heart of an empire that would last a thousand years.

## THE RISE OF THE NAZIS

The collapse of the economy in 1929 led many Germans to support the Nazis. Like Hitler, they believed that the crisis could be blamed on Jewish bankers. In January 1933, Hitler was made chancellor (prime minister). A month later, the parliament, the *Reichstag*, was burned down. The Nazis blamed the communists for the fire, but it is almost certain that they started it themselves. In the panic that followed, Hitler and his Nazi militia, the *Sturm-Abteilung* (SA), gave themselves greater powers, which they used to force people to support them.

In June 1934, Hitler had SA leaders killed, because he said that they were trying to overthrow him. He used his henchmen, the *Schutz-staffel* (SS), to do this. When the president, Hindenburg, died in August 1934, politicians and the army gave Hitler total power.

*The burning of the Reichstag*

## LIFE UNDER THE NAZIS

In the 1930s, Hitler was supported by most Germans, because his promises gave them back the pride that they had lost in the war. The Nazis used propaganda to win support. A minister for information, Joseph Goebbels, controlled all media and education. Once in power, the Nazis put into practice anti-Semitic policies. There were campaigns of violence against Jews and their property. Jewish shop windows were smashed and 35,000 Jews were arrested.

*A Nazi officer standing in front of a vandalized Jewish shop*

*The annual Nuremburg rally, where Nazis joined and celebrated*

The eagle was used as a symbol of strength and nationalism.

The swastika, adopted by Hitler as the Nazi emblem

Hitler made a speech at each rally.

Goebbels was in charge of organizing the rallies.

Young girls joined the League of Maidens.

Supporters of Nazism saluted one another with a raised hand and the words "Heil Hitler".

German boys joined the Hitler Youth, where they learned Nazi ideas.

Children swore an oath of loyalty to Hitler.

# International tensions of the 1930s

In the 1920s and 1930s, it looked more and more unlikely that peace in Europe would last for long. The treaties that followed the First World War had failed to resolve the political and economic rivalries that had started it. The situation worsened as certain European governments came under the control of aggressive fascist parties, seeking to extend their nation's power and influence.

## ATTACK ON ABYSSINIA

The Italian leader Mussolini promised to make Italy a strong world force. He wanted to distract the Italian people from economic problems at home by carrying out a successful foreign policy. In 1935, Italy went against the terms of the League of Nations by invading the African state of Abyssinia (now Ethiopia). Half a million Italian troops, armed with modern weapons, defeated the Abyssinian forces in just seven months. By May 1936,

*Emperor Haile Selassie*

Addis Ababa, the capital, had been captured. Haile Selassie, the ruler of Abyssinia, appealed to the League of Nations for support. The foreign ministers of Britain and France agreed to impose some limited sanctions on Italy. These consisted of a ban on trade and arms sales, but not on oil. These measures failed to stop Mussolini, and, by the end of 1936 Abyssinia was fully occupied by Italian soldiers.

*An Abyssinian soldier*

## GROWING GERMANY

After the First World War, Germany was surrounded by small weak republics. From 1933, Adolf Hitler was leader, and he promised to make his country great again. One of his first actions as chancellor was to withdraw from the League of Nations. He then attacked the Treaty of Versailles, which had been imposed on Germany after the War. In March 1935, conscription was re-introduced and the German army quickly doubled in size.

In March 1936, Hitler ignored the terms of the Treaty of Versailles and moved 20,000 troops into the German Rhineland. Other European countries failed to intervene because they did not want to risk a major dispute. Hitler's invasion had succeeded and his popularity further increased.

At this point Mussolini allied with Hitler, as a leader with similar aims. Together they planned to create an "axis" across Europe, which would be at the heart of a new world regime. Italy and Germany became known as the Axis Powers.

## THE SPANISH CIVIL WAR

Growing discontent with the monarchy in Spain led to the abdication of King Alfonso XIII in 1931. The king was then replaced by a democratic republic, but it proved weak. In 1936, the Spanish Civil War broke out.

*Spanish people celebrating the republic in 1931*

*The Spanish artist Pablo Picasso painted Guernica (below), to show his horror at the Nationalist bombing of a small town.*

The army, led by Generals Mola and Franco, attacked the socialist government. They were supported by the Catholic Church, right-wing politicians and Spain's fascists, the *Falange*. The war was fought between these right-wing groups, called Nationalists, and Republicans, the supporters of the government. The USSR gave the Republic limited support, while Britain and France avoided all action. Individuals from around the world rushed to defend the Republic, in groups called International Brigades, but they were no match for trained armies.

The Nationalists had a big advantage, as they were supported by other fascists and industrialists abroad. Mussolini sent troops and ships, and Hitler sent planes, crack regiments and tanks. The Spanish Civil War brought Mussolini and Hitler closer together and showed their military strength. In 1939, the Nationalists won the war and Franco became the dictator of Spain until his death in 1975.

## ASIA

During the 1930s, Japan, the most developed power in Asia, invaded and conquered parts of the nearby countries of Manchuria and China (see page 17). The growing power of the army drew Japan closer to fascist governments in Europe. In 1934, Japan made an anti-Soviet pact with Germany.

## ANSCHLUSS

By 1937, the terms of the Versailles settlement had been broken and Britain and France appeared to be unable to do anything about it. Hitler wanted to unite all German-speaking lands under his control and so proposed a union between Germany and Austria called the *Anschluss*. Schuschnigg, the chancellor of Austria, was forced by Austrian Nazis to call a referendum, in which the people would vote for or against a union. On March 11, 1938, before the referendum could take place, Nazi troops were sent into Austria. Two days later, Hitler declared the country part of the German Reich.

## CZECHOSLOVAKIA

By 1938, Czechoslovakia was the last surviving democracy in eastern Europe. With a German-speaking minority, natural resources and industries, it was an obvious target for Hitler's ambitions. In 1935, Germans there formed a group called the Sudenten German Party.

*A Czech anti-fascist poster*

Hitler encouraged the group to demand privileges from the Czech president, Eduard Benes. The French and British governments advised Benes to give Hitler what he wanted. The British prime minister, Neville Chamberlain, believed that by satisfying these demands another war could be avoided. This policy is known as appeasement.

Czechoslovakia's fate was decided at a conference held at Munich, Germany, in 1938.

*Chamberlain holding the paper, which claimed "peace in our time" after talks with Hitler in 1938.*

Hitler was given Sudentenland, the German-speaking area of Czechoslovakia, but by 1939 he had taken over the rest of the country too. France and Britain began to re-arm, but did not take military action, for fear of provoking a major conflict.

*This cigarette card shows how to put on a gas mask.*

## INVASION OF POLAND

The events of 1939 showed that Chamberlain had been wrong to assume that Hitler would stop at Czechoslovakia. After the Munich conference, Hitler focused his aggression on Poland, which had only recently been recreated from territory lost by Germany, Russia and Austria-Hungary after the First World War. Britain and France agreed to support Poland in the event of a German invasion.

Despite their ideological differences, the Soviet leader, Stalin, calculated that an agreement with Germany might lead to a division of Poland between the two countries. He had little faith in the abilities of France and Britain to resist Hitler. In 1939, the Molotov-Ribbentrop pact was signed between Germany and the USSR. This removed the final obstacle. On September 1, German forces invaded Poland. Chamberlain made a last attempt to avoid a conflict by suggesting a conference, but this failed. Two days later, France and Britain declared war on Germany.

*The Polish army used horses against modern German tanks.*

# The Second World War

The Second World War broke out on September 3, 1939, when the British and French governments declared war on Germany. In the early stages, the French and British were committed to a defensive war only, and were reluctant to fight on foreign soil. The Germans, on the other hand, fought aggressively and succeeded in capturing a number of smaller countries at great speed. Until 1942, it certainly seemed likely that they would win. But these early successes were reversed when the war spread to the USSR, Africa and the Pacific (see pages 28-29).

## BLITZKRIEG

In the early stages of the war, Germany used a new military tactic, known as *blitzkrieg*, meaning "lightning war" because of its speed. Blitzkrieg enabled the Germans to smash through foreign territory, securing quick victories. In doing so, they saved limited German resources. In the first month of the war, German forces, assisted by troops from the Soviet Union, succeeded in defeating Poland. The Soviet Union then invaded Finland, in order to gain territory to strengthen its military position. Apart from this, however, there was little activity on land during the winter of 1939. This period is often described as the "phoney war".

*Finnish soldier fighting on skis*

## RULING THE WAVES

As soon as war was declared, fighting began in the Atlantic, and continued for the whole of the conflict. German submarines and planes attacked the Royal Navy (the British navy), destroying Allied food supplies from British colonies. It was not until 1944, when the Allies captured German Atlantic bases, that this threat ended.

## INVASION OF FRANCE

In April and May 1940, Germany successfully invaded the nearby countries of Norway, Denmark, Belgium, France and Luxembourg.

On May 17, German forces broke through the Maginot line, a series of forts protected by heavy guns and anti-tank devices, which stretched along France's border with Germany. In an attempt to protect their people and land from more death and destruction, the French government surrendered to Germany on June 22. This surrender left many Allied troops trapped in northern France. Despite heavy bombing, the Royal Navy helped over 300,000 soldiers escape to safety in Britain from the beaches at Dunkirk.

From June 1940, half of France, was under direct German occupation with thousands of troops stationed there. The rest of the country was ruled by a pro-German government established at Vichy, a popular resort town in central France. The Vichy government was led by the French military leader Marshal Pétain, and the area was known as Vichy France.

*Map showing the partition of France*

*Allied soldiers swam to safety at Dunkirk.*

## BLITZKRIEG TACTICS

*This illustration shows the four stages of blitzkrieg, the German strategy that was so successful at the beginning of the war.*

**Stage 1**
The Luftwaffe (the German air force) bombed enemy territory.

Junker Ju 87B-1

**Stage 2**
Parachutists were dropped behind enemy lines to try to secure important positions.

Once the parachutists landed, they collected strategic information.

German planes dipped when bombing to improve their aim.

Railways, bridges and airfields were targetted in order to destroy communications.

## THE BATTLE OF BRITAIN

In June 1940, Mussolini, the Italian dictator, brought Italy into the war on Germany's side. This left Britain heavily outnumbered. Germany planned an invasion of Britain, codenamed "Operation Sealion", involving boat landings on the south and east coasts of the island, backed by air bombings. The British responded by building up their air force (the Royal Air Force, or RAF). By August 1940, it had over 500 new planes.

In August and September that year, British and German planes fought in an air battle which is known as the Battle of Britain. The German government was determined to take control of the air, as this would clear the way for a successful invasion of Britain. It was therefore crucial for the Allies to defeat them. The *Luftwaffe* attacked airports, factories and towns, but after many battles was defeated by the RAF.

*A British plane used in the Battle of Britain*

The Luftwaffe then started to bomb British cities at night. Many civilians were killed and large urban areas were destroyed. In 1941, the British retaliated and began an even more devastating bombing campaign of German cities and civilian areas.

## THE EASTERN FRONT

In October 1940, the Italians invaded the Greek mainland. In response, Britain sent forces to nearby Crete. The Germans came to the Italians' aid and, in April 1941, Hitler conquered Crete, Yugoslavia and parts of Greece.

Throughout the war, the Soviet leader, Stalin, took over more and more territory. By mid-1940, the USSR had annexed Latvia, Estonia and Lithuania. At the same time, the Germans believed they needed *lebensraum* ("living space") for their population and to supply raw materials and cheap foreign workers. The grain-producing area of Ukraine, in the Soviet Union, was a target for these ambitions.

Hitler's non-aggression pact with Stalin did not stop him from attacking the USSR. On June 22, 1941, German forces invaded the Soviet Union in an assault code-named "Operation Barbarossa".

*This Soviet poster claims to show the way German soldiers behaved.*

It was an enormous military action, with 200 divisions of soldiers, 3500 tanks and 3000 aircraft.

By December 1941, German forces had almost reached Moscow, but the Russian winter forced them to retreat south. Fighting began again in the spring. In June, German and Russian forces fought a long hard battle at the city of Stalingrad (now Volgagrad). The Soviet troops surrounded and defeated the German army. By directing too many resources to the Eastern front, Hitler had made a fatal error.

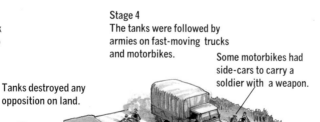

**Stage 3**
The heavy air attack allowed the tanks to break through into enemy territory.

Tanks destroyed any opposition on land.

**Stage 4**
The tanks were followed by armies on fast-moving trucks and motorbikes.

Some motorbikes had side-cars to carry a soldier with a weapon.

*Hot air balloons floated over London, holding up ropes to trap German bombers.*

# From Pearl Harbor to Hiroshima

War in the Far East had actually begun in 1937, when Japan conquered Chinese coastal areas (see page 17). The outbreak of a war in Europe in 1939 left the colonies of conquered European countries open to Japanese invasion and domination. The Japanese government hoped to turn the war to its advantage by joining the Axis Powers. In September 1940, Japan signed a pact of support with Italy and Germany.

## PEARL HARBOR

Initially the USA had little intention of joining the war, although the government offered US destroyers to help the Royal Navy destroy German U-boats in the Atlantic (in return for the lease of some British naval bases in the West Indies).

The decisive turning point in the war came on December 7, 1941. Without any warning, 360 Japanese aircraft bombed the American naval base at Pearl Harbor, Hawaii, causing enormous damage to US fleets. Outraged by the bombing, the USA, Britain and nine Latin American states declared war on Japan the following day. The bombing had a dramatic effect on the eventual outcome of the war, as it brought much-needed US resources to the aid of the Allies.

By June 1942, the Japanese controlled most of the Pacific area: Malaya, parts of Burma and Thailand, Indo-China, Hong Kong, the Dutch East Indies and the Philippines.

*The bombing of Pearl Harbor*

## WAR IN THE DESERT

From 1940, Allied and Axis forces also fought in North Africa. Hitler sent out troops to the Italian colony of Libya, under the command of Erwin Rommel. The Germans were successful at first but, in November 1942, British troops were victorious at the Battle of El Alamein and from then on never lost again. Later that month, US troops landed in Algeria. The Germans found themselves surrounded and were forced to surrender in May 1943.

*Tank and motorcycle divisions driving to the desert front*

## INVASION OF ITALY

The end of war in Africa left the Allies free to pursue an invasion of Italy. In July 1943, Allied troops successfully invaded the island of Sicily, close to the Italian mainland. After this defeat, the Italian people lost faith in Mussolini's leadership. His regime was so weakened that he fell from power. The Italian king, Victor Emmanuel, asked an army commander, Marshal Badoglio, to form a new government. Peace was made in September between the Allies and the new Italian leaders. Mussolini was rescued by a German commando raid, and made head of a small Nazi controlled republic called Salo, in northern Italy.

The Allies continued advancing north through Italy to challenge the German forces. Despite strong German resistance, they eventually captured Rome in June 1944, although German forces still remained north of the capital.

## D-DAY

The fighting in Italy was partly an Allied attempt to distract Hitler from their invasion of France (codenamed "Operation Overlord"). It was the largest amphibious (land and water) operation in history, with 5000 ships and 14,000 aircraft carrying 100,000 troops. On June 6, 1944 (known as D-Day), Allied forces landed on the beaches at Normandy after crossing the Channel from England. German leaders expected the invasion, but they had not learned where it would be, so they constructed forts along the whole of France's northern coast. It took the Allies over a month to break the German forces at Normandy. Eventually, Paris was liberated on August 25.

*This is the American B-17, or "Flying Fortress", which took part in bombing raids on German cities.*

Guns trained against enemy planes

Pilot and co-pilot

Glass nose to help the accuracy of the raid

## GERMANY SURROUNDED

From the end of 1944, Allied forces successfully advanced on Germany

By spring 1945, Germany was surrounded on all its borders.

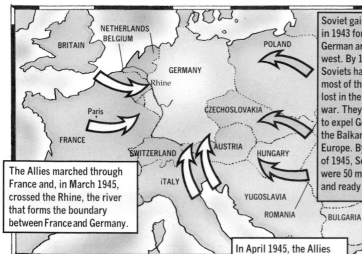

The Allies marched through France and, in March 1945, crossed the Rhine, the river that forms the boundary between France and Germany.

Soviet gains at Stalingrad in 1943 forced the German armies to retreat west. By 1944, the Soviets had taken back most of the land they had lost in the early years of war. They then went on to expel German forces in the Balkans and Eastern Europe. By the beginning of 1945, Soviet troops were 50 miles from Berlin and ready to invade.

In April 1945, the Allies advanced through Italy to Lombardy, a region close to the German border.

## GERMANY SURRENDERED

On April 8, 1945, Mussolini was shot dead by Italian communists, while attempting to escape to Switzerland. His body was then taken to be displayed in Milan. Two days later, realizing that Germany was defeated, Hitler committed suicide. Germany surrendered on May 8, 1945, known by the Allies as VE Day.

Two side guns

Bomb weighing about 4000kg (3.9 tons)

A gunner sat in this tiny glass bubble.

Allied bombings caused the destruction of many German cities, including Hamburg, Essen, Berlin and Dresden.

## WAR IN THE PACIFIC

Fighting with Japan continued, as the Allies moved all their troops and equipment to the Pacific in order to win the war. The Japanese government had overreached itself, and was finding it difficult to defend all its territories. Throughout May, June and July 1945, almost all the major cities in Japan were bombed by the US Air Force. In Tokyo, the capital, 80,000 people were killed in just one night.

*British troops advancing in Mandalay.*

At the same time, British and Commonwealth troops staged land attacks on the Japanese in Burma. The campaigns were destructive, but not decisive.

## THE ATOMIC BOMB

Since 1942, the Allies had secretly been developing an atomic bomb, which they hoped would force the Japanese to surrender. In August 1945, US planes dropped atomic bombs on the Japanese cities of Hiroshima and Nagasaki. The bombs killed over 150,000 people and led to terrible long-term damage from radiation.

On August 8, the USSR declared war on Japan and invaded Manchuria. This aggression, and fear of more atom bombs, led to complete Japanese surrender on August 14, 1945.

*An atomic bomb exploding*

# Aspects of war 1939-1945

The Second World War is sometimes described as a "total war" because it affected whole nations: their economies, their industries and their peoples. It is estimated that the conflict led to the deaths of 50 million people, of which over half were civilians.

## THE HOME FRONT

The war involved sacrifice for people on the home front. In Britain, for instance, food rationing was introduced, which meant that basic items, like milk and eggs, were restricted and imported foods, like coffee, chocolate, tea and bananas, were no longer available. As in the First World War, women filled the jobs that soldiers left. Some worked on farms and in industry, while others went to the war front, usually as nurses.

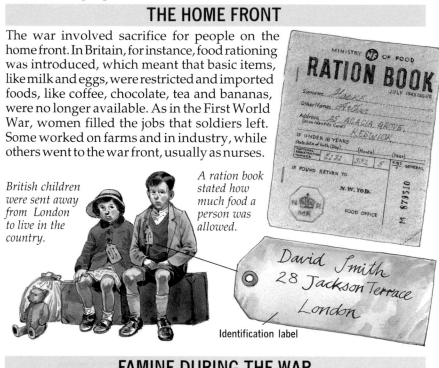

*A ration book stated how much food a person was allowed.*

*British children were sent away from London to live in the country.*

Identification label

## FAMINE DURING THE WAR

In some occupied countries, locally produced food was taken away to support fighting German soldiers. This led to famine, especially in Greece, Holland and Poland, where many people starved. This starvation was most acute in Warsaw, the capital of Poland, where thousands died in the Jewish quarter, known as the ghetto. As so many men were fighting at the front, the German government became short of workers for industry and agriculture. They began to round up people from occupied countries, in order to send them to Germany to work. Near the end of the war, the shortage of workers became so severe that the Nazis began to conscript children.

*Polish children were made to work for the Germans.*

## OCCUPIED COUNTRIES

Most people in occupied countries tried to live their lives as normally as possible and to protect their families. But there were two alternatives to this: collaboration (actively working with the occupiers) and resistance (fighting to rid the country of the invaders).

Active resistance groups had formed in most occupied countries by 1943. They produced newspapers, helped Jews and prisoners-of-war to escape, and spied on the occupiers. By giving military and geographical information to the Allies, they helped their armies to invade and expel the occupying forces.

After the war, members of the Resistance, such as General de Gaulle of France, were hailed as heroes, while those who had collaborated were punished. Some were executed, others were publicly humiliated.

*The French girlfriends of German troops were shamed by having their heads shaved and being paraded in the streets.*

## THE FINAL SOLUTION

According to Hitler, Jews, gypsies, homosexuals and the mentally ill were unworthy of a place in the German empire. Hitler wanted to get rid of them in a plan known as the Final Solution. From 1941, the Nazis built huge prisons, called concentration camps, in German-occupied countries. Hitler used these camps to carry out his plan. They were turned into places of murder, where at least 12 million people were poisoned in gas chambers, shot, or starved to death.

There was a tradition of prejudice against the Jews in Europe. Nazi policies took advantage of this anti-Semitism to make the Jews suffer. *Holocaust*, a Greek word meaning "total destruction", is used to describe the deaths of about six million Jews during the war. Of three million Jews in Poland, only half a million survived. The full horror of Hitler's camps was revealed to the world when the Allies marched into them in 1945. Many could not believe that such a terrible thing had been allowed to happen.

*These are the gates of the Auschwitz camp, where 12,000 people were gassed every day.*

# WAR TECHNOLOGY

The demands of the Second World War led to advances in aircraft, flying bombs and weaponry. One of the most widely used inventions was the sub-machine gun, an automatic light weapon which could be carried and fired by just one man. In the 1930s, both sides developed jet-powered planes which could go much faster than those powered by propellers. Perhaps the most important inventions of all were those of the German scientist Wernher von Braun. In 1944, he developed the V-1, a flying jet-powered bomb. The following year, his team built the V-2, a jet rocket which could hit and destroy a target from a distance of 320km (200 miles). These were launched on Britain from German-occupied countries in Europe.

Ways of defending countries also improved, both before and during the war. By 1939, Britain had a chain of radar stations along its southern and eastern coasts. These used radio waves to detect aircraft up to 160km (100 miles) away. They were vital in preventing a successful air attack and invasion of Britain.

The atomic bomb, the most powerful weapon yet developed, was used at the end of the war. The death and devastation caused was so terrifying that an atomic bomb has not been used in war since. The fear of nuclear war has dominated politics in the second half of the century.

*Radar equipment like this was vital for defending Britain from a planned German invasion.*

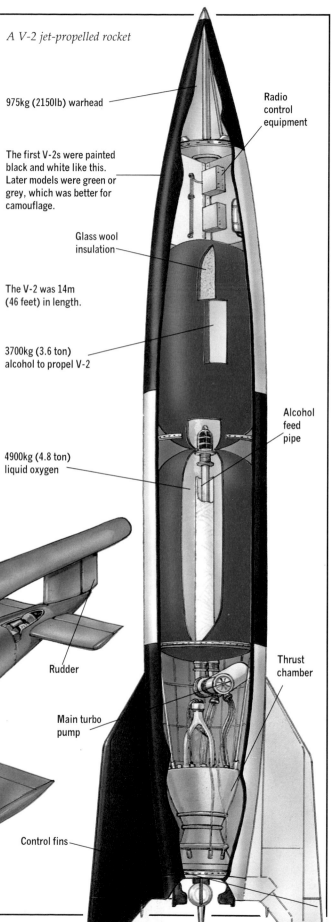

*A V-2 jet-propelled rocket*

975kg (2150lb) warhead

Radio control equipment

The first V-2s were painted black and white like this. Later models were green or grey, which was better for camouflage.

Glass wool insulation

The V-2 was 14m (46 feet) in length.

3700kg (3.6 ton) alcohol to propel V-2

Alcohol feed pipe

4900kg (4.8 ton) liquid oxygen

Thrust chamber

Rudder

Main turbo pump

Control fins

*A V-1 flying bomb*

Wings

The V-1 did not need a pilot.

Magnetic compass to steer V-1

Small propeller

850kg (1870lb) of explosives

# Problems of the post-war world

The Second World War has had an enormous influence on international politics in the second half of the 20th century. The entry of the USA and USSR into the war had been decisive in bringing about an Allied victory. As a result, these two nations grew in strength, while the old European powers declined in importance.

## THE BIG THREE

Most of the decisions involving the peace treaties were made by Winston Churchill (the British prime minister), Josef Stalin (the Soviet leader) and Franklin Roosevelt (the US president). These men were known as "the big three".

*Churchill, Roosevelt and Stalin at Yalta*

In August 1941, Roosevelt and Churchill first met to negotiate plans for post-war settlements. To try to prevent future wars and promote world peace, they agreed to set up an international organization, rather like the old League of Nations (see page 10). In January 1943, the two leaders discussed the best way of ending the war quickly.

There were two more conferences in Tehran and Cairo in November that year. Among other points, it was decided that US forces should occupy Japanese territory in the event of an Allied victory. This was because they had the biggest military presence in the Pacific.

## CONTINUED CONFERENCE

In February 1945, the big three came together again at Yalta, on the Black Sea. Stalin insisted that the USSR keep almost all the Polish territory that had been seized in 1939.

Churchill and Roosevelt were pressured into agreeing to these demands, because Stalin already had such a large number of troops in Poland.

The incident increased tensions between the leaders. The distrust of the USSR by the West, especially by the US government, was by now very well-established.

*The new map of Germany*

Berlin
Potsdam ⊕

GERMANY

Occupation zones
☐ British
☐ French
▨ Russian
☐ US

Vienna ⊕
AUSTRIA

## THE LAST WORD

The very last meeting between the Allies took place at Potsdam in Germany, within months of the German surrender in May 1945. Britain had a new prime minister, Clement Attlee, and the United States had a new president, Harry Truman. Stalin, the old man of the Allied conference, dominated the decision making.

*Attlee, Truman and Stalin at Potsdam*

As a result of discussions in Potsdam, Germany and Austria were divided into four zones controlled by the Allies. Italy lost territory to Yugoslavia, while the other Axis Powers in Europe lost territory to the USSR. Over the next 25 years, Soviet influence over eastern and central Europe grew.

## THE UNITED NATIONS

The United Nations (or UN) was set up in San Francisco in 1945. It required all its members to contribute armed forces to serve as peacekeepers when requested and to protect nations under attack. By 1970, the four original members (the USA, Britain, the USSR and France) were joined by almost every country in the world.

*The UN headquarters in New York*

*This poster advertises the United Nations.*

## THE COLD WAR BEGINS

Since its foundation in 1917, the USSR had been distrusted by the non-communist powers. Alliances formed during the war meant that the USSR and the USA had to work together. But, without a common enemy, rivalries between the West (the USA and allies) and the East (the USSR and allies) were rekindled. In 1947, the US government sent troops to Greece to fight communist guerillas there. The USA also issued the Truman Doctrine, by which they offered US support to any groups fighting communism. The struggle between the East and West became known as the Cold War (see pages 48-9).

## MARSHALL AID

After the war, the US government wanted to help rebuild the economies of non-communist countries in Europe . It was hoped that this would preserve democracy and prevent the spread of communism, as well as providing a market for American goods. The Secretary of State, George Marshall, introduced a scheme known as the Marshall Plan, by which millions of American dollars were poured into European countries.

*Poster advertising Marshall aid*

## THE SUPERPOWERS

In 1949, the western allies reacted to the threat of communism by forming a military alliance called the North Atlantic Treaty Organization (NATO). The USSR retaliated in 1955 by forming the Treaty of Friendship, Co-operation and Mutual Assistance, known as the Warsaw Pact, which was signed by all the countries under Soviet influence. The creation of these two alliances highlighted the divisions between the two superpowers: the USA and the USSR.

## BERLIN

The differences between East (Soviet-controlled) and West (non-Soviet) Germany became more obvious with the introduction of Marshall aid, especially in the divided city of Berlin, which was inside East Germany. The French, British and US sections of the city merged to form West Berlin and grew much richer than the Soviet sector.

In June 1948, the Allies introduced a new currency into West Berlin. Stalin felt that this represented the building of a permanent non-communist area inside East Germany. On June 23, the Soviets closed all rail and canal links to the city from the West. This is known as the Berlin blockade. The Allies reacted with the Berlin airlift. For 328 days, US planes flew supplies into West Berlin. On May 12, 1948, the Soviets lifted the blockade because they did not want to risk provoking a war.

In 1949, East Germany was officially named the German Democratic Republic. The western part became the Federal Republic of Germany.

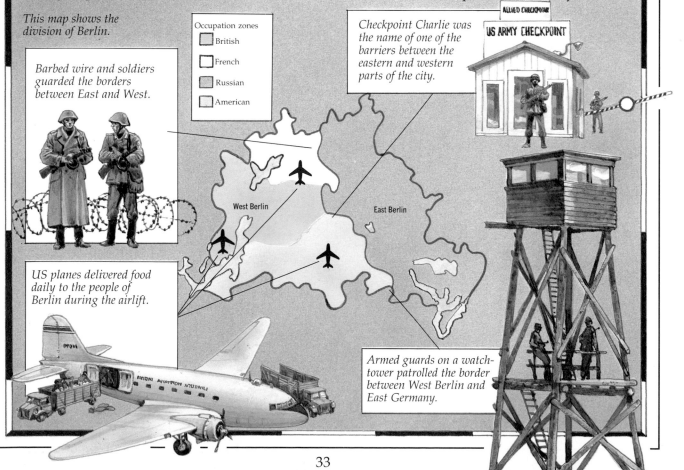

*This map shows the division of Berlin.*

Occupation zones
- British
- French
- Russian
- American

*Barbed wire and soldiers guarded the borders between East and West.*

*Checkpoint Charlie was the name of one of the barriers between the eastern and western parts of the city.*

ALLIED CHECKPOINT

US ARMY CHECKPOINT

West Berlin

East Berlin

*US planes delivered food daily to the people of Berlin during the airlift.*

*Armed guards on a watch-tower patrolled the border between West Berlin and East Germany.*

# Science and technology

Until this century, most scientists worked independently. But the rising cost of equipment and the growing complexity of scientific research has meant that today most scientists work in teams. Projects are funded by industries and governments, who expect research to have practical applications. As a result, rapid technological advances have been made in areas such as warfare, transport and space exploration.

## TECHNOLOGY IN EVERYDAY LIFE

It was not until the 20th century that petroleum, electricity and oil became widely available as sources of power. During the first decades of the century, electric lighting was installed in houses in Europe, the USA and other developed nations. Streets became safer as they were better lit. Heating from oil and electricity, rather than by wood or coal, was used for the first time. In some countries, new time-saving devices were introduced, such as vacuum cleaners, refrigerators and washing machines, giving people more time and freedom.

*This picture shows a 1930s kitchen with some of the new time-saving appliances.*

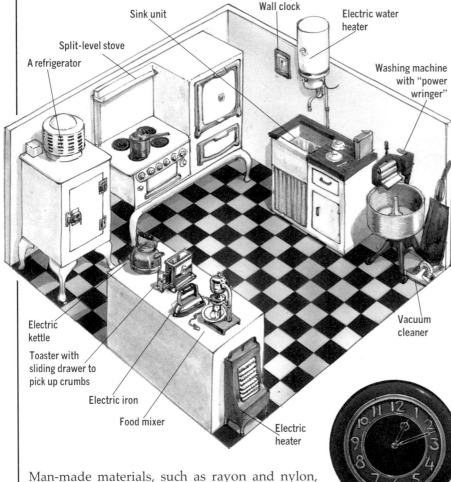

Wall clock

Sink unit

Electric water heater

Split-level stove

A refrigerator

Washing machine with "power wringer"

Electric kettle

Toaster with sliding drawer to pick up crumbs

Electric iron

Food mixer

Vacuum cleaner

Electric heater

Man-made materials, such as rayon and nylon, were developed and used for the first time in electrical appliances and household goods. Plastics, such as Bakelite (invented in 1907) and PVC (first sold in 1943), were introduced into industrial processes, packaging and the home. They soon became an essential part of modern life.

*This 1930s clock is cased in Bakelite plastic.*

## PHYSICS

In the late 19th century, many scientists believed they were on the point of discovering a complete explanation of the universe and how it worked. They described matter in terms of tiny, indivisible particles called atoms, using the classical laws of physics, drawn up in the 17th century by Isaac Newton, to explain their movement. But new revelations suggested that atoms contained even smaller particles, as well as large amounts of energy.

Max Planck, a German physicist, suggested that energy does not travel in continuous waves, but is made up of tiny particles, or "quanta", of energy. He coined the term "quantum physics" to describe this study.

*Albert Einstein*

In 1905, German-born scientist Albert Einstein published his revolutionary Relativity Theory. This overturned Newton's system of fixed measurements of time and motion. He showed that all motion is relative; that all we can measure is how fast we are moving in relation to something else. He stated that the only fixed constant in the universe is the speed of light. He expressed the relationship between mass and the energy of moving objects in the equation $E=mc^2$.

*The example of a moving car has been used to demonstrate the theory of relativity.*

To the people standing still, the car is moving.

To the person in the car, the people appear to be the ones who are moving.

## ATOMIC STRUCTURE

At the end of the 19th century, scientists discovered negatively charged particles inside atoms, which they called electrons. To help understand atoms, physicists built "models", which do not look like the insides of atoms, but make their properties clearer. Ernest Rutherford, a New Zealander, showed that atoms have a small hard core or nucleus, about 10,000 times smaller than the atom itself. Neils Bohr, from Denmark, worked with Rutherford on developing a new model of the atom, incorporating all their discoveries. During the 1930s, some researchers explored the internal structure of the nucleus itself.

An electron occurs in each of these "clouds".

*One of the latest models of the inside of an atom*

Some of the greatest European scientists were German Jews. But because of Hitler's persecution of the Jews, many of them left Germany and German-occupied lands for Britain and the USA. These scientists believed that it was essential for the USA to build an atom bomb before Germany did, so that, in the event of war, their weapons would be more powerful. With their help, the American military forces directed a research plan, known as the Manhattan project, to produce an atomic bomb. As a result of their work, two atom bombs were dropped on Japan at the end of the Second World War.

*This bomb was called "fat boy" and was dropped on Nagasaki, Japan. in 1945*

After the war, work in atomic physics focused on the tiny particles which arrive from outer space in cosmic rays. This science was particularly important in the USA in the 1960s. US scientists invented a device called a bubble chamber, which enables a photographic record to be made of fast-moving particles. Scientists began to discover and classify many more tiny sub-atomic particles, such as quarks.

*Silver balloon used for investigating cosmic rays*

## NEW SOURCES OF POWER

The use of electricity has increased throughout the 20th century. Today, large amounts of coal and oil are burned to generate this power, which has led to widespread pollution. People have searched for a cleaner alternative. From the 1950s, scientists built on the research that went into the atom bomb to develop nuclear electricity. It was promoted as a way of generating electricity, while conserving limited natural resources. But a safe way of dealing with the products of nuclear waste has not been found. Another disadvantage of nuclear fuels is the possibility of an accident, called a meltdown. This happens when the walls of the reactor melt, releasing radioactive

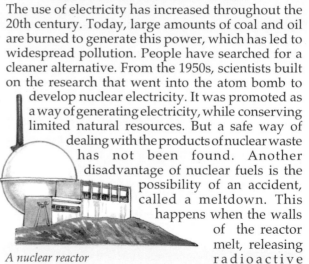

*A nuclear reactor*

material into the atmosphere. In 1986, a huge meltdown occurred at Chernobyl in the Ukraine (then a province of the Soviet Union). This disaster caused radiation to spread over a large area of northern Europe. Other safer methods of creating power from natural and unlimited resources, such as sun, wind and water, have been encouraged. In the 1970s, solar panels were developed, but the high cost of installation and their low power output have limited their use.

*A solar-powered telephone in a hot Middle Eastern country*

Two layers of silicon

Light from the Sun

The Sun causes electron movement between the two layers, causing electricity.

More successful has been hydroelectric power (HEP), generated by the flow of water from reservoirs. In 1990, a fifth of all the world's electricity came from HEP stations.

*A hydroelectric power station*

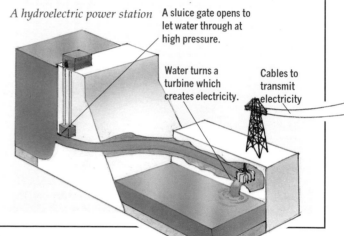

A sluice gate opens to let water through at high pressure.

Water turns a turbine which creates electricity.

Cables to transmit electricity

# Biology and medicine

Throughout the 20th century, biological discoveries have led to improved health and longer life expectancy. More is known about the importance of vitamins and minerals in the diet, and the effects of chemicals, such as hormones, on the body's activities. New products such as chemical fertilizers have also resulted in better food supplies.

## SPREADING CULTURE

One of the greatest innovations in 20th century medicine was the introduction of antibiotics, drugs used to combat infection caused by bacteria. In 1928, the British scientist Alexander Fleming became the first person to notice that the culture penicillin could successfully prevent the spread of a bacteria. In 1941, two other chemists, Henry Florey and Ernst Chain, isolated the active ingredient in it and pioneered the use of purified penicillin as an antibiotic. It was of immediate use in treating those wounded in the Second World War, and can be used in almost all medical treatments.

*A Penicillin culture*

*Alexander Fleming*

## DIAGNOSIS OF DISEASE

X-rays (waves of energy which travel through flesh) were first discovered in 1895 by the German scientist Wilhelm Röntgen. They enabled doctors to see inside a patient's body for the first time and became useful for diagnosing diseases and then trying to cure them.

*X-ray photograph of a human hand*

In 1955, fibre optics, which carry light along strands of flexible glass, were developed. This led to the production of the endoscope, a flexible telescope, which examines inside the body.

*Fibre optics are used in endoscopes to examine inside a patient's body.*

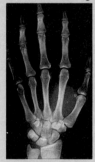

Guiding and watching it through a magnifying glass

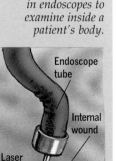

Endoscope tube

Internal wound

Laser beam

## TRANSPLANT SURGERY

Great advances have been made in surgery. The treatment of almost every part of the body has undergone a radical change. New drugs developed in the first decade allowed doctors to control their patients' pain and consciousness far more accurately. Transplant and artificial replacement surgery is another 20th century development. From the 1940s, kidney dialysis machines were used to perform the functions of a healthy kidney. In the 1950s, doctors went one step further by performing the first successful kidney transplants.

*Drugs to numb feeling are injected into the blood.*

*Pain-killing tablets and pills*

*A 1960s kidney dialysis machine*

It was not until 1967, however, that the first human heart transplant operation was carried out. Over the next two decades, many more heart transplants were done, but many of the patients died when their bodies rejected their new hearts. The problem of rejection has still not been entirely overcome, but more patients are surviving the operation. An alternative to transplant surgery is a cardiac pacemaker, which was first made in 1958. This machine is fitted internally and stimulates a weak heart with tiny electric shocks.

Electrode leading to heart

Pacemaker

Heart

*This cardiac pacemaker is implanted next to the heart and sends electric shocks at a rate of 80 beats a minute.*

## PREGNANCY AND PREVENTION

In the 20th century, more effective ways of preventing pregnancy have been discovered. The most reliable is the oral contraceptive, known as the pill, which was introduced in the 1960s. Its use increased women's freedom, but people worried as more became known about its side effects. There have also been developments in helping infertile women have children. *In vitro fertilization* (IVF) was first carried out in 1978. The female ovum is first fertilized in a test-tube, and so children produced by IVF are known as test-tube babies.

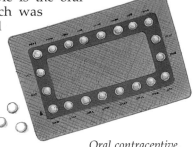

*Oral contraceptive, known as the pill*

## GENETICS

The term "gene" was first coined in 1909 to refer to the factor which decides which characteristics are inherited by a particular animal or plant. Later, the chemical DNA (deoxyribonucleic acid) was isolated as the key to this code, although its structure remained a mystery. After 1945, research on DNA was carried out in Britain by Francis Crick, Rosalind Franklin, James Watson and Maurice Wilkes. Their work led to the discovery of the structure of DNA in 1953. Crick and Watson built a large model of the complex DNA molecule as two chains of chemicals wrapped around each other and joined at points by chemical bonds. This shape is called a double helix. A consequence of this discovery was the development of "genetic engineering", the altering of the characteristics of an organism by changing its DNA code. Genetic engineering has enabled substances, such as human insulin for treating diabetes, to be produced in a laboratory.

*The double helix structure of DNA*

Chemical bonds linked in pairs

*Crick and Watson with their model of DNA*

## MODERN PLAGUES

There are illnesses that medicine cannot cure. Cancer is a big cause of early death in the western world. Although many forms of the disease can be treated with chemotherapy (courses of strong drugs), surgery and radio-therapy (treatment by radiation), many types of cancer remain incurable.

In 1982, a new disease called AIDS (Acquired Immune Deficiency Syndrome) was identified. A person suffering from AIDS loses the immune system which defends the body against the spread of viruses and bacteria. The disease has become a serious problem all over the world and no cure has yet been found.

*A poster warning of the dangers of AIDS*

## PSYCHOLOGY

Psychology, the study of how the mind works, did not become a widely applied science until the 20th century. The Austrian scientist Sigmund Freud (1856-1939) used the term "psycho-analysis" to describe his methods of recovering hidden memories from patients. His aim was to understand problems in patients' thoughts or actions. He described the mind in terms of different levels of understanding.

Carl Jung (1875-1961), one of Freud's pupils, made a study of dreams which led to his theory of "collective unconscious". He believed that everybody shares a knowledge of past human life, which is expressed in dreams.

The Russian scientist Ivan Pavlov, working in the 1900s, studied the way dogs behaved and concluded that animals and humans could be trained to react instinctively to an event. This is known as conditioning.

*These diagrams show Pavlov's experiments.*

The dog's mouths automatically watered, or salivated, at the sight of food.

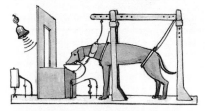

Pavlov rang a bell when the dog ate, so that it associated the bell with food.

Soon the dog salivated every time the bell rang, even if it was not given food.

# Asia and decolonization

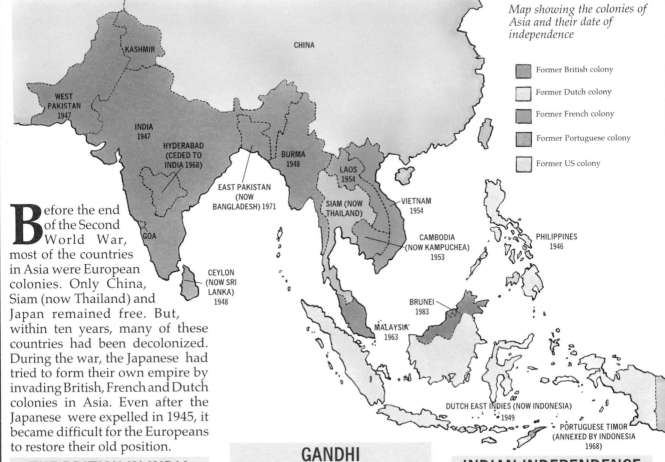

*Map showing the colonies of Asia and their date of independence*

KASHMIR

CHINA

WEST PAKISTAN 1947

INDIA 1947

HYDERABAD (CEDED TO INDIA 1968)

BURMA 1948

LAOS 1954

EAST PAKISTAN (NOW BANGLADESH) 1971

SIAM (NOW THAILAND)

VIETNAM 1954

GOA

CAMBODIA (NOW KAMPUCHEA) 1953

PHILIPPINES 1946

CEYLON (NOW SRI LANKA) 1948

BRUNEI 1983

MALAYSIA 1963

DUTCH EAST INDIES (NOW INDONESIA) 1949

PORTUGUESE TIMOR (ANNEXED BY INDONESIA) 1968

- ◼ Former British colony
- ◻ Former Dutch colony
- ◼ Former French colony
- ◼ Former Portuguese colony
- ◻ Former US colony

**B**efore the end of the Second World War, most of the countries in Asia were European colonies. Only China, Siam (now Thailand) and Japan remained free. But, within ten years, many of these countries had been decolonized. During the war, the Japanese had tried to form their own empire by invading British, French and Dutch colonies in Asia. Even after the Japanese were expelled in 1945, it became difficult for the Europeans to restore their old position.

## THE BRITISH IN INDIA

British power in India had been growing since the 18th century. By the late 19th century, most of India was under their control. After the First World War, however, the British economy was weakened and the empire became increasingly difficult to maintain. Western ideas of democracy and the right of a country to rule itself became popular and pressure for self-government grew.

The two main religious groups in India, Hindus and Muslims, began forming separate political organizations, with the aim of fighting for Indian independence.

*A parade of elephants in colonial India*

## GANDHI

From 1920, the biggest nationalist group, the Indian National Congress (INC), was led by Mohandas Gandhi, an Indian lawyer. He became known as the *Mahatma*, which means "the great soul", for the wisdom and courage he showed in his opposition to British rule. He encouraged Muslims and Hindus to work together to weaken British authority. He attracted support for his campaign of civil disobedience and non-violent resistance.

*Mahatma Gandhi*

## INDIAN INDEPENDENCE

In the face of so much opposition, it became impossible for Britain to maintain its position, especially after it had been weakened by the Second World War. As independence became more and more likely, disagreements broke out between the different religious groups. The Muslims, under the leadership of Mohammed Ali Jinnah, wanted a separate state for themselves. Gandhi strongly believed that the whole of the sub-continent should be united, but violence between the two groups began to grow.

_Rioting in India between Hindus and Muslims in 1931_

Buildings belonging to rival religious groups were set on fire.

Hindus and Muslims attacked each other.

## DIVISIONS

Faced with the prospect of a civil war, the British government granted independence to separate states in 1947. The bulk of the area became a mainly Hindu state, called India. A Muslim state called Pakistan was created to the north. Ceylon, an island to the south of India, was given independence and later renamed Sri Lanka. But the violence continued, as many people were not living with the rest of their religious group. Thousands were uprooted, as Muslims moved north to Pakistan and Hindus moved south to India. During this mass migration, fights broke out between the groups. Many people were killed and villages destroyed. Gandhi himself was murdered by a Hindu extremist in 1948.

_Muslims from Hindu areas flocking to Pakistan_

Political violence between Muslims and Hindus continued long after independence. Further tensions were caused by Sikhs, a religious group based in the Indian region of Punjab, who wanted a separate state of their own. In Sri Lanka, a group of Hindus called Tamils also struggled for independence.

Indira Gandhi (the daughter of India's first leader, Jawaharlal Nehru) was prime minister for most of the 1960s and 1970s. She was shot in 1984 by one of her bodyguards, a Sikh extremist. Her son and successor, Rajiv Gandhi, was killed in a bomb explosion in 1990.

_Rajiv Gandhi_

Between East and West Pakistan lay large areas of Indian territory. Power was concentrated in the West. In 1971, East Pakistan broke away from West Pakistan. A brutal civil war erupted and thousands were killed. The conflict only came to an end when Indian troops joined the war and ejected West Pakistani soldiers from the East. The state of Bangladesh was then created.

Sri Lanka also suffered unrest. A civil war between Tamils, (originally from southern India) and other Sri Lankans (mainly Buddhists) has raged since 1970.

## STATE OF INDEPENDENCE

Once India had its independence, it became difficult for the European powers to maintain control in the rest of the continent. Some Asian nationalists, for instance in the Dutch East Indies, hated European rule so much that they had sided with their Japanese occupiers in the Second World War.

One by one, the colonial powers withdrew from the area: the USA from the Philippines in 1946, the British from Burma in 1948 and, after a bitter war, the Dutch gave up Indonesia (formerly Dutch East Indies). In 1957, Malaya was given independence and six years later expanded to form Malaysia.

_A celebratory military parade in Malaysia in 1957_

## WAR IN INDO-CHINA

The process of decolonization in French Indo-China was especially difficult and violent. The French lands consisted of the ancient kingdoms of Cambodia, Laos and Vietnam. During the Second World War, communists led by Ho Chi Minh became very popular with poor Vietnamese peasants and helped to expel the Japanese.

When the French tried to resume rule in 1945, a jungle war broke out between them and Ho Chi Minh's forces. The French army was eventually defeated and, by 1954, the three kingdoms were declared independent.

_Medal celebrating the 50th anniversary of French Indo-China_

# Africa and decolonization

D uring the 1880s, in a period of rapid colonization known as the Scramble for Africa, virtually all of the continent was taken over by European powers. Between 1947 and 1975, however, most countries were freed from foreign rule. This process of decolonization often involved conflict, war and bloodshed, both against the colonial powers and between rival nationalist groups. Many African states have been economically and politically unstable ever since.

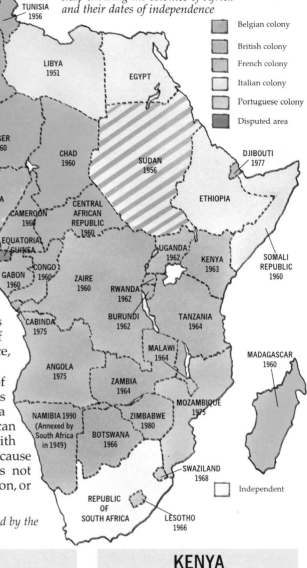

*Map showing the colonies of Africa and their dates of independence*

Belgian colony
British colony
French colony
Italian colony
Portuguese colony
Disputed area

MOROCCO 1956
TUNISIA 1956
WESTERN SAHARA
ALGERIA 1962
LIBYA 1951
EGYPT
MAURITANIA 1960
MALI 1960
SENEGAL 1960
GAMBIA 1965
GUINEA BISSAU 1974
NIGER 1960
CHAD 1960
SUDAN 1956
DJIBOUTI 1977
GUINEA 1958
BURKINA FASO 1960
TOGO 1960
BENIN 1960
NIGERIA 1960
CENTRAL AFRICAN REPUBLIC 1960
ETHIOPIA
SIERRA LEONE 1961
IVORY COAST 1960
CAMEROON 1960
SOMALI REPUBLIC 1960
LIBERIA
GHANA 1957
EQUATORIAL GUINEA
UGANDA 1962
KENYA 1963
GABON 1960
CONGO 1960
ZAIRE 1960
RWANDA 1962
CABINDA 1975
BURUNDI 1962
TANZANIA 1964
MALAWI 1964
MADAGASCAR 1960
ANGOLA 1975
ZAMBIA 1964
MOZAMBIQUE 1975
NAMIBIA 1990 (Annexed by South Africa in 1949)
ZIMBABWE 1980
BOTSWANA 1966
SWAZILAND 1968
Independent
REPUBLIC OF SOUTH AFRICA
LESOTHO 1966

## AFRICAN UNITY

The modern map of Africa has so many straight lines because it was drawn up by European powers, without any regard to traditional tribal boundaries. Groups of people are often scattered across several state boundaries and many countries are made up of a large number of different tribes or language groups. In Nigeria, for instance, over 200 different languages are spoken.

Many Africans supported the idea of Pan African Unity, in which nations would be independent, but united in a federation. The Organization for African Unity (OAU) was founded in 1963, with the aim of promoting alliances. But because of long-term disagreements, it has not been successful in achieving federation, or effective in preventing disputes.

*This picture shows African soldiers employed by the British to help enforce their rule.*

## EARLY DECOLONIZATION

Egypt became independent from Britain in 1922, but the main phase of African decolonization began in the late 1950s. Many Europeans had delayed the process because they felt that African people were not capable of governing themselves. In 1957, Ghana became the first black African country to become independent. British politicians believed that Ghana was ready for self-rule because it had an educated leader, Kwame Nkrumah, and natural wealth.

A number of other African colonies soon followed Ghana's lead (see map). In 1960, the British prime minister, Harold Macmillan, spoke of the "winds of change" blowing across the continent.

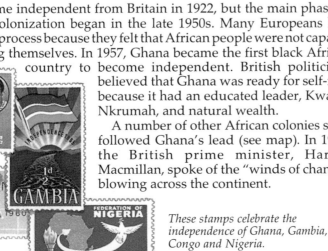

*These stamps celebrate the independence of Ghana, Gambia, Congo and Nigeria.*

## KENYA

Although the British withdrawal from Africa was generally peaceful, violence broke out in Kenya in the 1950s. A secret movement, the Mau Mau, used violence against the British in an attempt to bring about change. The British forces reacted harshly. Thousands were killed, both by the Mau Mau and by the British.

*Jomo Kenyatta, first Kenyan president*

## RHODESIA

In 1964, Southern Rhodesia was denied independence by Britain because white Rhodesians refused to give political rights to the black majority. In 1965, whites, led by Ian Smith, declared that Rhodesia was no longer a colony and that they intended to take control. Blacks formed two nationalist groups, ZANU and ZAPU, which used guerilla tactics against the government.

After a decade of violence, Smith agreed to black rule. In 1980, Rhodesia was made independent and renamed Zimbabwe.

*Ian Smith*

## ALGERIA

In Algeria, nationalist demands were rejected by the white French settlers, who had lived there since the 1840s. According to the French constitution, Algeria was actually part of France, but its Arab people were never given political rights. Algerian Arabs formed the National Liberation Front, which fought the French in an eight year colonial war. Independence was finally granted in 1962.

## THE CONGO CRISIS

In 1960, Belgium suddenly withdrew from the colony of Congo (now Zaire). The people were unprepared for this, and it was followed by civil war between ethnic groups. The unrest, known as the Congo Crisis, lasted until 1965. The United Nations sent a large army to restore order.

*UN troops in the Congo*

## PORTUGAL AND ITS COLONIES

Despite the changes in the rest of Africa, the Portuguese government was determined to keep its colonies. From 1950, nationalist groups in Mozambique, Guinea Bissau and Angola used guerilla tactics against their Portuguese rulers. Finally the colonies were granted independence after the fall of Portugal's military dictatorship in 1975.

The years of fighting had left the new countries in ruins. Independence was followed by terrible civil wars in Angola and Mozambique, which continued well into the 1990s.

*The flags of Mozambique, Angola and Guinea Bissau*

## SOUTH AFRICA

In 1910, South Africa was given dominion status, under the rule of a white minority, who formed less than 20% of the population but held all power. The whites were divided between Afrikaners (those of Dutch origin who spoke a language called Afrikaans) and English-speaking people. In 1949, *apartheid* (meaning "separateness"), was introduced. The population was divided into four groups: white, people of mixed race, black and those of Asian origin. Public places, such as schools and beaches, had one section for whites and another for non-whites.

*An example of apartheid*

To avoid giving black people the vote, the whites set aside certain areas of the country for them. The areas, usually poor in resources, were known as homelands, or *bantustans*. The government was able to claim that blacks had a vote in their own independent states. In fact, the states were economically dependent on South Africa and were not recognized by other governments.

The African National Congress (ANC) had been formed in 1912, to try to change the situation in South Africa. After the introduction of apartheid, their membership grew. Strikes and demonstrations were organized and there were attacks on whites. The government responded with harsh measures and many of the ANC activists were imprisoned or executed. Nelson Mandela, one ANC leader, was imprisoned for almost 30 years.

In 1985, in the face of economic sanctions from abroad and violence at home, the government began to reform. By 1991, many of the apartheid laws had been abandoned. People were no longer divided into racial categories, blacks and whites were allowed to live in the same areas, and the ANC was legalized.

*Nelson Mandela*

*An ANC poster demanding equal rights for black people*

# Israel and Palestine

The area sometimes called the Holy Land is important to three religious groups: Christians, Jews and Muslims. Because of this, it has long been the scene of war and bloodshed .

A Jewish kingdom was founded in 1000BC, but it was taken over by the Romans in 63BC and renamed Palestine. In AD636, the region was conquered by Muslim Arabs and, in 1517, by the Ottoman Turks. As a result of Muslim rule, many Jews left and settled throughout the Middle East, North Africa and Europe. In their new homes they were often persecuted as outsiders.

## ZIONISM

In 1896, a movement called Zionism was formed by Jewish leaders in Europe. The aim of Zionists was to establish a Jewish homeland, and many began to emigrate to the Holy Land. By 1914, there were 90,000 Jews in Palestine, living alongside half a million Arabs.

*Theodor Herzl wrote this, the first Zionist book.*

## BRITISH INVOLVEMENT

During the First World War, much of the Middle East was occupied by the British. After the war, the League of Nations gave Britain control of Palestine, Trans-Jordan and Iraq.

In 1917, the British issued the "Balfour Declaration", expressing support for Zionism. In protest against Jewish immigration, Palestinians rioted in 1929 and 1936. In 1937, Britain put forward a partition plan, by which Palestine would be divided into a Jewish state, a larger Arab state and an area controlled by Britain. But the Arabs rejected it. To try to reduce Arab opposition, Britain issued a law halting Jewish immigration.

The Nazi anti-Semitic policies led to more support for a Jewish homeland. Jews were angry that they were refused entry into Palestine at their time of greatest need, and many fled there illegally.

## THE CREATION OF ISRAEL

After the Second World War, as the full horror of Nazi atrocities was revealed, demands for a Jewish homeland became stronger. In 1947, Britain turned to the United Nations for a solution. The UN drew up a plan to divide Palestine into an international area, an Arab state and a Jewish state. But this plan was rejected by the Palestinians and the other Arab states.

British control of Palestine ended on May 14, 1948. Zionist leaders immediately declared the formation of a Jewish state, named Israel. The following day, Arab armies from Egypt, Iraq, Syria, Jordan and Lebanon invaded to crush Israel. But the Israeli troops halted the Arab advance.

*The Holy City of Jerusalem*

*David Ben-Gurion, Israel's first prime minister*

In 1949, a ceasefire agreement was declared, by which Israel retained more former Palestinian territory than it had been given in the original UN partition plan. Jerusalem was divided into two, with Jordan controlling the eastern half of the city. Jordan also took charge of the West Bank, a central region of the country along the banks of the River Jordan, while Israel occupied western Jerusalem. The name Palestine disappeared overnight from the map of the Middle East.

LEBANON
SYRIA
Arab territory seized by Israel in 1948-9
Golan Heights
Israeli border
MEDITERRANEAN SEA
River Jordan
Jerusalem
Gaza Strip
ISRAEL
JORDAN
SINAI
EGYPT

*This map shows Israeli territory in 1949.*

Mohammed, the Muslim prophet, is said to have risen to heaven at the Dome of the Rock.

The Wailing Wall, where Jews worship

## REFUGEES

In 1948 and 1949, 600,000 Palestinians fled from their homes in the newly created Israel. Some were forced to leave by Israeli troops. Others believed they would be safer in Arab areas, although most of the countries they went to did not offer them citizenship or a home. About 160,000 Arabs stayed in Israel, where they were treated as second class citizens.

At the same time, life became harsher for Jews living in Arab countries. As a result, many Jews fled to Israel and the number of Jews there doubled in a few years.

*Palestinian refugees*

## THE SUEZ CRISIS

When President Nasser came to power in Egypt in 1952, he encouraged Palestinians to attack Israelis. In 1956, he provoked more tension by seizing control of the Suez Canal. The Canal was jointly owned by Britain and France, and it was crucial to European and Israeli trading routes. Israel sent forces into Egypt, while France and Britain sent troops to the canal zone to regain control of it. This led to worldwide protest and the troops were withdrawn in 1957.

## THE SIX DAY WAR

For the next 10 years, tension between the Arab states and Israel remained high. In 1967, Nasser stationed troops on the Israeli border. Israel, fearing an attack by Arab forces, attacked first. The Israelis destroyed the Egyptian Air Force and invaded Syria. In the conflict, known as the Six Day War,

Israel captured the Sinai region and the Golan Heights, as well as the Gaza strip, the West Bank and east Jerusalem, areas populated by over a million Palestinian Arabs.

## THE YOM KIPPUR WAR

On October 6, 1973, Egypt and Syria launched a surprise attack on Israel. It was Yom Kippur, an important Jewish holy day, and most Israelis were attending the synagogue. At first, the invading armies made rapid gains, but Israel fought back. The USA and the USSR both wanted influence in the Middle East. The USA supplied arms to Israel and the Soviet Union supplied the Arabs. After three weeks of heavy fighting, a ceasefire was agreed.

*Israeli F4E plane*

## TALKS AT CAMP DAVID

In 1979, US president Jimmy Carter helped to set up a peace conference in Camp David, USA, attended by the Egyptian president, Anwar Sadat, and the Israeli leader, Menachem Begin. They agreed to establish diplomatic relations between the two countries. Israel agreed to withdraw from Sinai, and Egypt agreed not to attack Israel.

The other Arab states were angry with Egypt for making peace and, in 1981, Sadat was assassinated by Muslim extremists.

*Camp David agreement being signed by Begin and Sadat, with Carter looking on*

## THE PLO IN LEBANON

In 1964, a group of Palestinian Arabs, led by Yasser Arafat, formed the PLO (Palestinian Liberation Organization). The PLO carried out terrorist attacks to draw the world's attention to the Palestinian plight.

From 1970, the PLO was based in Lebanon. In an attempt to drive them out, Israeli troops invaded Lebanon in 1982. The troops became involved in a civil war between Lebanese Christians and Muslims. Their involvement led to world protest and Israeli troops were withdrawn in 1983.

*This PLO poster says "Smash Israel".*

*Yasser Arafat*

## TOWARDS PEACE

At the end of 1987, Palestinians in the West Bank and Gaza launched a violent uprising against Israel. Despite continuing tension between Palestinians and Israelis, and more attacks on Lebanon, positive steps toward peace have been taken. In 1993, the Israeli government and the PLO recognized each other's status, and negotiated with it, making a lasting agreement more likely.

*Israeli Centurion tanks moving into the West Bank*

# Trains, planes and automobiles

At the beginning of the century, there were only 9000 cars on the world's roads, and nothing in the sky but clouds, birds and the occasional hot-air balloon. Advances in travel have been rapid and dramatic, transforming the way people live, their surroundings and their knowledge of the rest of the world. As well as improvements in 19th century forms of travel, entirely new types of vehicles have been invented, from helicopters to hydrofoils. Travel is getting faster and more efficient all the time.

## TRAINS

In the first half of the century, there were few advances in railway travel, because many people saw cars and planes as the transport of the future. But, from the 1960s, the efficiency of passenger trains was improved so that they were more able to compete. The first of these new high-speed trains was the Japanese *Shinkansen*, known as the bullet train. It runs on an electrified track at a speed of over 200km (125 miles) per hour. In 1981, the French government introduced its *Train à Grande Vitesse* (TGV) which travels at almost 400km (250 miles) per hour.

*The TGV and Bullet trains*

## CARS

*A 1903 Cadillac Model-A*

In 1900, cars were very expensive and very slow. But over the century, cars became much cheaper, faster and lighter, as lighter metals and plastics were used in their manufacture. By 1950, there were over 40 million cars in the USA alone. This increase in car ownership came largely as a result of the mass-production techniques started by the American Henry Ford (see page 14). By the 1990s, there were almost 500 million cars in the world, and this figure is set to rise even further. Although cars are useful, they have also brought with them problems of pollution and road congestion.

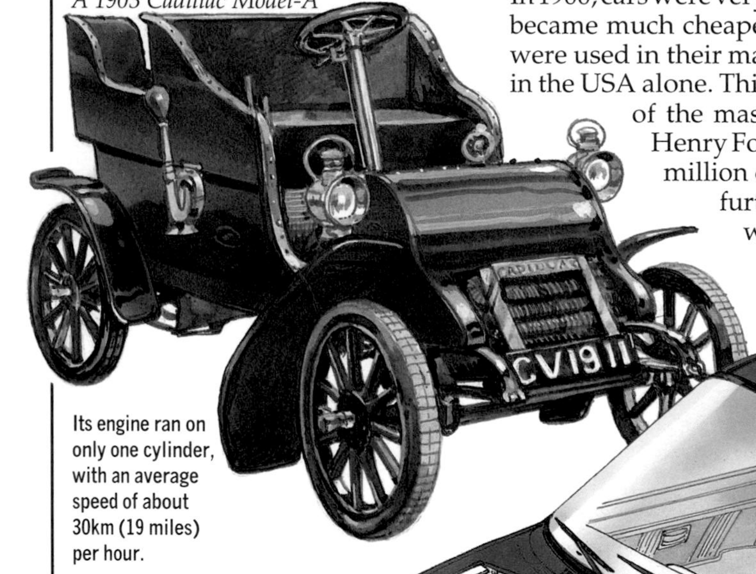

Its engine ran on only one cylinder, with an average speed of about 30km (19 miles) per hour.

*A 1993 Fiat Cinquecento, a typical modern, small car*

Light metal frame

Plastic bumper

Catalytic converter, which filters fuel

90% of the poisons are filtered out of the fuel.

# PLANES

*The Boeing 747-400, Concorde and the Wright brothers' first plane are shown here to the same scale.*

In 1903, the Wright brothers made the first powered flight in *Flyer 1*, which was made of wood, wire and fabric. The number of planes grew rapidly, because of their value in the First World War. In 1949, jet passenger planes were introduced, leading to cheaper flights. The *Boeing 747* (or jumbo jet), which can hold up to 500 passengers, first flew in 1969. Seven years later, the French and British governments introduced *Concorde*, which travels faster than the speed of sound.

The narrowness of Concorde's wing span is designed to make it more aerodynamic. This means it travels faster through the air.

The whole distance flown in the first powered flight is the same as the length of the economy class in a 747.

Double wings

Flight deck where two pilots sit

The angle of the wings is designed to make the plane more efficient.

Jet engines

The nose of Concorde droops forward during take-off and landing to improve the pilot's view.

## HELICOPTERS

At the turn of the century, Paul Cornu of France built a craft with rotating blades, which barely lifted itself off the ground. In 1939, the Russian-American inventor Igor Sikorsky designed what is considered to be the first modern helicopter. It had a single main rotor, could take off and land vertically and move in any direction.

*Sikorsky's machine and a modern helicopter*

## UNDER AND OVER THE SEA

In the 20th century, there have been fewer improvements in marine travel than in land travel. In 1900, the Italian Enrico Forlanini built the first hydrofoil, a boat which is raised out of the water by wings under the hull. This helps to lessen friction and make it travel faster. Even more efficient is the air cushioned vehicle (ACV), which makes a cushion of air between the craft and the sea. It was invented in Britain in 1955 by Christopher Cockerell. The first nuclear-powered submarine was also introduced in 1955. It could travel nearly 100,000 km (62,000 miles) without refuelling and was used for both naval and scientific purposes.

Propellers to power the craft

*A modern air cushioned vehicle, used for short sea crossings*

Skirt

To move forward, the "skirt" lifts up and traps air underneath.

F or 40 years, Europe was divided by an "iron curtain", which lay between the communist and non-communist states. The two zones were known as the Eastern and Western blocs. The division began in 1945, when Soviet troops had marched into many of the German-occupied countries and dominated the area. In 1955, the East was united in an agreement called the Warsaw Pact.

*Map showing Warsaw Pact countries*

## EAST GERMANY

In 1949, the Soviet occupied zone of Germany was named the German Democratic Republic (GDR). Although officially independent, Soviet troops were stationed there and the government followed Soviet policies. After the war, food shortages and poverty led to rioting against the regime. Many people escaped to the West in search of a better standard of living. To try to stop this flow of refugees, the government of the GDR built the Berlin Wall (see page 48).

*East Germans burning the Soviet flag*

## HUNGARIAN REVOLUTION

The 1947 elections in Hungary were won by communists who followed Stalinist policies. In 1953, a liberal communist called Imre Nagy became party leader and began to introduce reforms. He was forced to resign by the USSR, but pressure for democracy continued.

In 1956, workers and students demonstrated in the capital, Budapest, demanding the total withdrawal of Soviet troops. In an attempt to end these protests, the Communist Party reinstated Nagy. But he refused to obey orders and instead pushed to make Hungary more independent. The Soviets sent tanks to crush the resistance. A pro-Soviet government was installed, and Nagy and his associates were

*In 1956, Soviet tanks rolled into Budapest to stop the anti-communist revolt.*

executed. This brief period of liberalization is known as the Hungarian Revolution. A pro-Soviet policy was followed until the 1970s, when liberal measures began to be introduced once more.

## THE PRAGUE SPRING

After the 1948 elections in Czechoslovakia, the communists became the largest party in the government. The new prime minister, Klement Gottwald, banned all opposition and refused Marshall aid. In 1968, a liberal called Alexander Dubcek became leader of the Czech Communist Party. He began to introduce laws to bring greater freedom. Popular protests broke out in support of Dubcek. But, in October, they were brutally put down by invading Soviet troops and tanks. Dubcek and his allies were removed from power and the period known as the Prague Spring was over.

Hungarian flag

Ordinary people armed themselves to challenge the Soviets.

Soviet tanks

This poster shows how people viewed the Soviets: as liberators and then oppressors.

## BULGARIA AND ROMANIA

In the 1940s, pro-fascist monarchies in Bulgaria and Romania were replaced by left-wing governments, which soon became allied to Moscow. Vulko Chervenkov became president of Bulgaria in 1950, introducing strict Stalinist policies. Romania was dominated by two leaders: Gheorghe Gehorghiu-Dej (1945-65) and Nicolae Ceausescu (1965-89).

## POLAND

After the war, Poland was taken over by communists supported by Stalin. Under their rule, food shortages and political restrictions led to protests. In the 1970s, martial law was introduced to end the unrest. This was opposed by the Catholic Church and the trade unions, and it was this opposition that brought down the government later (see page 68).

Soviet troops and commanders

## STALIN AND THE USSR

Josef Stalin continued as leader of the USSR until his death in 1953. Stalin believed that post-war recovery would come by reviving the system of Five Year Plans, which set high production goals for armaments factories and heavy industries. These strict policies resulted in a rise in production, but the lives of the peasants and workers did not improve.

This Soviet author, Alexander Solzhenitsyn, was exiled from the USSR in 1974.

The board game Monopoly was banned in the USSR because of its capitalist theme.

The government's control of other areas of life was equally strong. All books, plays and films were banned if they showed any signs of anti-Soviet influence. The security forces and the police had unlimited powers. Those who were suspected of anti-Soviet activity or thought were sent to harsh prison camps, called *gulags*.

After Stalin's death, the USSR was ruled by a group of politicians in a "collective leadership". But, by 1956, Nikita Khrushchev had emerged as leader. He launched a series of attacks on Stalin's reputation, describing him as a tyrant who had built up a "cult of personality". His policies, known as destalinization, led to greater freedom in the USSR. More uncensored films and books were released but, despite these reforms, any book or form of art that criticized the revolution or seemed Western in influence was banned.

Khrushchev's economic policies concentrated on agriculture. Unused land was farmed and new crops were introduced, but these policies did not improve food supplies. He also attempted to change the way the Communist Party was run. This angered other politicians who thought that he was trying to build his own cult of personality. In October 1964, Khrushchev was removed from office by a group of rivals, who had the support of the army.

## STAGNATION

In the late 1960s, Leonid Brezhnev emerged as the most powerful politician in the USSR. Under his leadership little changed; critics of the regime, called dissidents, were still imprisoned and there was hardly any economic growth. This is known as the period of stagnation.

Leonid Brezhnev

## DECLINE OF COMMUNISM

Yuri Andropov, who became leader in 1982, introduced a radical plan of reform to make the communist system more efficient. But he soon became ill and the reforming process ended. When he died in 1984, one of Brezhnev's allies, Konstantin Chernenko, was chosen as his successor. But he died too, after only a year in office. His replacement, Mikhail Gorbachev, had worked with Andropov and built up support in the party to push through rapid reforms which changed the world (see page 68).

# The Cold War

The Cold War is the name given to the tension and hostility that developed between the USA and the USSR after 1945. Both sides built up their nuclear forces and supported struggles between communist and anti-communist groups elsewhere.

## THE KOREAN WAR

After Japan's surrender in 1945, Korea was divided into two areas: the Soviet-occupied North and US-occupied South. By 1949, the superpowers had withdrawn their troops, but the divide remained. In 1950, Koreans in the North invaded the South to re-unify the country. The United Nations sent troops and, by the end of the year, occupied almost all of Korea. China did not want such a close US presence, and sent troops into Korea. This led to a war that went on for two years, causing the deaths of three million Koreans. After all this, the UN decided that the country should remain divided.

*This map shows the division of Korea.*

## THE BERLIN WALL

After the division of Germany, many people from communist East Germany fled to the richer West through the Allied sector of Berlin (see page 33). By 1961, about 20,000 people were escaping every month. To prevent further escapes, the Soviets built a huge wall between the two sectors. Thousands were shot and killed trying to get over it.

*The building of the Berlin Wall*

## CUBA AND GRENADA

In 1959, Fidel Castro set up a socialist regime in Cuba. This worried the US government, as it was so close to their own coast. At the Bay of Pigs in 1961, Castro defended the island from an attack by US-supported Cuban exiles.

Two years later, US planes saw Soviet ships unloading weapons there and missile sites being built. The US president, John F. Kennedy, demanded that Soviet missiles be removed from the island. Tension was so great that the world seemed to be on the brink of a nuclear war, but the Soviet leader, Khrushchev, agreed to remove the missiles. In return, the USA promised not to invade Cuba. But they continued to carry out expensive operations to try to break the Castro regime.

In 1983, a revolutionary military council seized power in Grenada. Believing that the coup was backed by Cubans, US marines invaded the island, to try to keep it free from Cuban influence. International protest led to the withdrawal of the troops, but the USA succeeded in getting rid of the military council.

*Photographic evidence, shown below, was used to prove that missile sites were being built in Cuba.*

*Kennedy (on the left) and Khrushchev in 1963*

## COMMUNISM IN VIETNAM

By 1954, Vietnam was independent from France (see page 39). It was divided into communist North Vietnam, led by Ho Chi Minh, and South Vietnam, which had a US-supported dictatorship under Ngo Dinh Diem. But Ho Chi Minh did not accept the division and sent troops to gain control of the South. He was aided by many southern peasants. Later, the US government sent forces to try to stop the spread of communism and the conflict developed into a full-scale war.

*Ho Chi Minh*

*The USA made extensive use of helicopters to get through the thick jungle during the Vietnam war.*

## THE VIETNAM WAR

By 1968, there were half a million US troops in Vietnam, assisted by forces from Thailand, South Korea, Australia, New Zealand and the Philippines. But they had little success against the Vietcong (communist guerillas), who were masters of jungle warfare. The US began to use desperate measures, spraying chemical defoliants over the country to kill vegetation, in an attempt to reveal guerilla hiding places. This damaged the long-term health of civilians and troops.

People all over the world were horrified by photographs and films of the war. Public criticism and lack of success led to US withdrawal in 1973. Two years later, the North Vietnamese successfully invaded the South, and reunited the country.

The Vietnamese jungle made air attacks more difficult.

A US UH-1B helicopter

A US marine firing on the ground

Vietnamese villages consisted of houses built of grass and straw.

## SPIES AND SPYING

During the Cold War, both sides built up a network to spy on the other. Activity revolved around two government bodies, the American CIA and the Soviet KGB. They both used the media in a propaganda war. The US portrayed communism as a grim threat to the American way of life. In the Soviet Union, all press was controlled by the state.

Batteries

Energy stores

Sensitive microphone

*This pen doubled as a bugging device used by spies.*

The jungle was sprayed with chemicals such as "Agent Orange". This made the leaves fall off the trees, improving visibility.

## DETENTE

The superpowers saw there were huge dangers in waging a constant, undeclared war, especially with the development of nuclear weapons. During the 1970s, there was an easing of tension known as *detente*. But the end of the Cold War was delayed when Soviet troops invaded Afghanistan in 1979. The action was condemned by the UN. The US president, Jimmy Carter, imposed tough sanctions and led a boycott of the 1980 Olympic games, held in Moscow, as a protest against the invasion.

Relations were strained further with the election of a new president, Ronald Reagan, who believed that communism was still a grave threat to the USA. Both sides put new, highly advanced, missiles in Europe. Reagan also threatened to put arms in space, with the "Star Wars" (Strategic Defensive Initiative) project. Despite this, a friendlier relationship began to develop between the powers.

*An Afghan rebel*

*This diagram shows Star Wars weaponry.*

Solar panels to provide power

Target sensor scanning Earth

Telescope pointing to Earth

The USA emerged from the Second World War stronger than before. In the following decades, the country played an enormous role in world politics, while dealing with domestic problems of racial tension and political corruption in high places.

President F.D. Roosevelt, who had governed the USA throughout the war, died in 1945 and was replaced by Harry S.Truman. The new president launched building and welfare schemes, in order to prevent mass unemployment for the 16.5 million returning soldiers.

## REDS UNDER THE BED

During the 1950s, the phrase "better dead than red" was used by Americans to express the hysterical fear that communism would destroy their way of life. Joe McCarthy, a Republican politician, led public trials (known as witch-hunts) against anybody suspected of being communist or "unAmerican". He attacked many in the military forces and the film industry, destroying some careers in the process. Government agencies promoted anti-communist films, literature and newspapers.

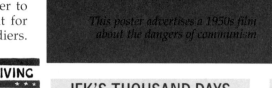

*This poster advertises a 1950s film about the dangers of communism*

*A poster celebrating US prosperity*

## EISENHOWER'S OFFICE

In 1953, and again in 1956, General David Eisenhower (popularly known as Ike) was elected as president. He tried to improve the post-war economy by selling off state businesses. The recent success of the Soviet space projects forced Ike to invest vast amounts of money into research into space travel.

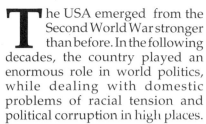

*Rockets like this one were built during Eisenhower's term of office.*

## JFK'S THOUSAND DAYS

In 1961, the Democratic candidate, 43-year-old John F. Kennedy, became the youngest elected president of the USA. His policies included medical care for old people, better state education and the promise that an American would be the first to walk on the moon. He also pumped money and men into wars in Cuba and Asia.

On November 22, 1963, Kennedy was assassinated in Dallas, Texas. The event shocked the whole world. An ex-soldier, Lee Harvey Oswald, was arrested, but was himself shot dead while in police custody.

*John Kennedy and his wife Jackie, moments before he was shot and killed.*

It is not known whether Oswald acted alone, or whether Kennedy's death was part of a plot, perhaps involving government agencies and the Mafia. Lyndon B. Johnson, the vice president, pushed through many of Kennedy's policies.

## RICHARD NIXON

In 1968, the Republican Richard Nixon became president. He tried to reduce crime and poverty, but cut back state spending on health and education. During his term there was unrest, especially in colleges, where students protested against poor social conditions and US involvement in Vietnam (see pages 48-9). Nixon used troops to put down demonstrations. In 1970, an anti-war protest at Kent State University ended in the fatal shooting of four students, when National Guard troops fired without warning. Despite such events, Nixon was re-elected in 1972.

*A protest march against Nixon's policies*

*Richard Nixon*

## THE WATERGATE SCANDAL

During the 1972 elections, there was a break-in at the Democratic Party headquarters, the Watergate Hotel. Sensational investigations by *The Washington Post* revealed that the men arrested for it had government connections. When tape recordings later proved that Nixon knew what was going on (in addition to owing over half a million dollars in taxes), he was forced to resign - the only president in US history to do so.

*Telephone bugging device used in the break-in*

## RECESSION IN THE USA

Gerald Ford, who succeeded Nixon, became president during a period of unemployment and inflation. His successor, Democrat Jimmy Carter, tried to reduce unemployment, and stressed the need for energy conservation to end US reliance on Arab oil. But the American public questioned his ability to manage the economy. In 1979, Carter became even more unpopular when he failed to free Americans held hostage at the US embassy in Iran (see page 73).

## THE REAGAN YEARS

In 1980, Carter lost the election to Republican candidate Ronald Reagan, an ex-film star from California. He reduced the role of government in social welfare and civil rights. Many people were wealthier than before, but there was also an increase in the number of very poor people. Reagan believed that communism still posed a frightening threat to the free world. To defend the USA, he spent more money on weapons and began an arms project, known as "Star Wars", in which missiles were to be based in space. Reagan won a landslide victory in the 1984 elections.

*Ronald Reagan*

## THE FIGHT FOR CIVIL RIGHTS

Although many African-Americans had died for their country in the Second World War, in parts of the USA black people were still seen as second class citizens. In the southern states, segregation was common in schools and on buses. Many tried to change the law, but failed in the face of deep-rooted resistance.

Truman ended segregation in the army and increased the number of black voters registered. Eisenhower tried to end segregation in schools. In 1957, he ordered that nine black students be admitted to a white school in Little Rock, Arkansas. Violence broke out as whites mobbed the school to stop the black students.

In the 1960s, the numbers joining groups fighting for black civil rights grew. In 1963, 200,000 protestors marched to Washington, where they were addressed by the civil rights leader Martin Luther King. He promoted the use of peaceful protest, and his speeches persuaded many to fight for black rights. In 1968, he was shot by a hired assassin. For the first time in US history, national mourning was declared for a black citizen.

Although all citizens were now officially equal, African-Americans were still much poorer. From 1965 to 1968, a series of riots broke out in black urban areas. More radical leaders, such as Malcolm X, preached the use of violence.

*A poster by the radical Black Panthers*

Civil rights protests carried on throughout the 1970s and 1980s. In May 1992, tensions exploded in Los Angeles when, despite video evidence to the contrary, four white policemen were found not guilty of beating up a black motorist. Riots broke out in the city and 58 people were killed.

*Protesters during the Los Angeles riots of 1992*

*National Guards tried to protect black students from being attacked by racists.*

*Martin Luther King*

# Art and architecture

Art and architecture have changed more radically this century than in any previous one. Painting moved away from exact representation and pure description (pictures of things) to work which was more about expressing thought and feeling (pictures about things). Groups of artists got together to share ideas and new forms of expression and their work formed art movements.

## EARLY ART MOVEMENTS

Expressionists and Fauvists, such as the French artist Henri Matisse, used bold hues and broader brushstrokes to express mood and emotion. Cubism was a movement started by Pablo Picasso and Georges Braque in 1907. Cubists tried new ways of solving the problems of painting three-dimensional scenes onto canvas. They produced paintings in which linear, broken-up images suggested a new kind of reality. They were called Cubists because of their use of straight lines and hard edges.

*"The Three Dancers" by Pablo Picasso*

Some artists chose not to represent the world around them. In 1911, Wassily Kandinsky produced the first "abstract" painting. From 1917, Piet Mondrian painted arrangements of vertical and horizontal black lines, with patches of red, yellow and blue. After the Second World War, US artists Jackson Pollock and Mark Rothko did not even paint lines. Pollock dripped and splashed paint onto the canvas.

## PRIMITIVE ART

Many of the great artists of the century were influenced by the "primitive" art of Africa, Central America and Indonesia. Sculptors such as Henry Moore and Barbara Hepworth used primitive forms to re-examine natural shapes and textures and give a new vitality to traditional art.

*"Family Group" by Henry Moore*

## THE SURREALISTS

In 1900, Sigmund Freud suggested that in dreams the mind reveals concerns usually hidden, or repressed. Surrealist artists tried to show what was inside the subconscious. Their pictures did not make sense if viewed in the same way as other art. Salvador Dali, Rene Magritte and Max Ernst, painted seemingly unconnected images in a precise, realistic style.

*The Spanish artist Salvador Dali*

## CONCEPTUAL ART

After 1945, "conceptual art" developed, inspired by the French artist Marcel Duchamp. Paintings, sculpture, film and arrangements of objects aimed to make people think about art. To conceptualists, the idea behind art is more important than the finished product. In the 1960s, Andy Warhol painted exact copies of cans of soup and Joseph Beuys filled an entire room with rolls of black felt.

Toward the end of the century, artists have chosen different ways to express themselves. Conceptual art has continued to make statements, while others have returned to more "realistic" ways of representing objects.

*"Rabbit" made in 1986 by Jeff Koons*

*Andy Warhol's "Marilyn" illustrates the way in which he used familiar images.*

# ARCHITECTURE

In the 20th century, new materials, such as concrete, plate glass and steel, have given architects more choice and flexibility. Many have tried to use this technology to create new types of building. Two great architects who began their careers in the 1900s were Frank Lloyd Wright in the USA and Peter Behrens in Germany. Both were very influential. Behrens wanted to make industrial buildings more efficient and attractive. His pupils went on to found the International Style. Wright concentrated on designing private houses and developed a style known as the Prairie House, with large, low rooms and wide entrances. This style influenced the design of houses in suburban areas, in the outskirts of cities. By the end of the century, half the population of the USA lived in suburban areas, often in houses inspired by Wright's ideas.

*"Falling Water" House, USA, designed by Frank Lloyd Wright*

## CURVES AND SHAPES

Some architects since the Second World War have reacted against the strictness of Modernism by using curved and irregular shapes, particularly in airports and stadiums, where large spaces have to be covered.

*The Sydney Opera House in Australia*

## SKYSCRAPERS

Skyscrapers are often seen as the typical 20th century building, although they were first constructed in the 1880s. After 1945, tower-blocks were presented as the brilliant solution to the problems of over-crowding in big cities. In practice they were not, as many people found them inhuman and inhospitable.

*The Trans-America Building in San Francisco*

## INTERNATIONAL STYLE

The most influential style of architecture this century has been Modernism, or the International Style. It was characterized by clean lines and right angles. In 1918, Walter Gropius formed the Bauhaus school in Germany, which brought together some of the most influential designers of the century. Their ideas developed into what is now called Modernism. The architects le Corbusier and Mies van der Rohe wanted to design large-scale, low cost housing for poor workers, using prefabrication and mass production.

*The Shroeder House in Holland was designed by Rietveld.*

## INSIDE-OUT

In the 1970s and 1980s, some architects emphasized the functional aspects of a building, which architects in the past had often tried to conceal. Richard Rogers, Renzo Piano and Michael Hopkins used polished steel or primary shades to highlight heating, air-conditioning, elevators and other services.

*The Lloyds building, in London, designed by Richard Rogers*

In 1900, Western music was dominated by the 500 year-old tradition of European art music (usually known as classical music). But, in the course of the century, new styles from many different cultures became popular.

## WESTERN ART MUSIC

In the 20th century, composers questioned the principles that had governed Western art music for hundreds of years. In the 1900s, the composers Gustav Mahler, Claude Debussy and Arnold Schoenberg were already experimenting with new ways of writing music. Their attitudes had a huge influence.

The Russian Igor Stravinsky is one of the century's most important composers. In 1913, he wrote the music for the ballet *The Rite of Spring*, which so shocked the audience that it caused a riot at its first performance. Other radical composers of the time included the Hungarian Béla Bartók and the Czech Leos Janácek.

The Austrian Arnold Schoenberg changed the order of notes to achieve new forms of expression. He introduced music based on rows of 12 notes, rather than scales of eight. His pupils Alban Berg and Anton Webern carried on this style, which later became known as serialism. It remains an important principle of 20th century art music and has been used by many composers in the second half of the century, including Luigi Nono, Luciano Berio, Pierre Boulez and Karlheinz Stockhausen.

*This cartoon shows Stravinsky conducting his angular music.*

## JAZZ AND BLUES

Jazz evolved in New Orleans, in the USA, in the 1900s. It contained elements of African-American music that had been brought over from Africa by slaves. By the 1920s, jazz had become very popular, particularly in Chicago, New York and New Orleans, as well as some cities in Europe. When musicians such as Louis Armstrong and Duke Ellington began recording in the mid-1920s, jazz began to reach an even larger audience.

*An early jazz band in the USA*

Another African-American style, blues, began in the south of the USA. As jazz became popular with white audiences, blues became popular in black urban areas. In the 1940s, it evolved into rhythm and blues, which used the electric guitar to great effect.

## SONGS AND SINGERS

At Tin Pan Alley, in New York, composers such as Irving Berlin and Cole Porter wrote popular songs. Publishers grew richer, as more people bought the music to these songs and recordings of them. Both the songs and the people who sang them reached a wide audience. Americans Frank Sinatra and Ella Fitzgerald were two of the first singers to achieve great wealth and fame as successful recording musicians.

*Frank Sinatra*

## ROCK AND ROLL

In the 1950s, rock and roll became a fashionable form of music in western countries. This new style took elements from rhythm and blues and from American country music. It was based around an electric guitar and drums, with strong simple rhythms. The recording companies that made rock and roll records aimed this music specifically at a young audience.

Although the word "teenager" (used to describe those aged between 13 and 19) was first coined in the 1920s, it was not until the 1950s that teenagers began to act as a separate group with particular ways of behaving. They had more money to spend on clothes and records than ever and businesses realized that there was a lot of money to be made out of them. The growth of recording and radio industries gave them the means to exploit this youth market.

*Elvis Presley*

# THE POP EXPLOSION

After rock and roll came a succession of pop, or popular, music styles. Each type of music has been associated with a particular image and lifestyle. In the 1960s, pop groups like the Beatles and the Rolling Stones became successful. Their music took elements from black American styles. The ideas expressed in their songs often reflected social attitudes of the time.

*A 1950s jukebox, which plays records in exchange for a coin*

*The Beatles in 1963. They were soon to become the world's most successful pop group.*

Pop music has become a huge industry, with a great influence over the lives and ideas of young people. Pop stars, such as Madonna and Prince, are among the most famous people in the world.

The growth of the pop industry in Europe and the USA has also led to an increase in the popularity of music from Latin America, India and Africa. Known as world music, it is often marketed and sold by western record companies. In the mid-1990s, however, many experts are predicting a huge drop in music sales to 13-21 year-olds (who traditionally buy a lot of records), as computer games rise in popularity.

*Madonna*

*Bob Marley sang reggae, which combines Caribbean and American styles.*

# TECHNOLOGY

The development of music has been closely linked to technological change. The first method of recording was invented by Thomas Edison in 1877. Sound was recorded onto a rotating cylinder. A decade later, Emile Berliner developed the disc phonograph, or record player. Sound was recorded on to a long spiral path on a rotating disc.

*An early cylinder phonograph*

Horn to amplifiy sounds

Wax cyclinder

*A 1903 Poulsen telegraphone, used for recording the human voice*

*A 1990s digital audio tape and a standard cassette*

Standard cassette

DAT

Throughout the century, the phonograph has been steadily improved, making it cheaper and more reliable. Mass production techniques mean that most people in the richer countries can afford to buy one. In the 1950s, records became cheaper and lighter than before. The expansion in the recording industry came as a result of technically improved records, the growth of the teenage market and the boom in youth music styles, like rock and roll. These forces combined to create a vast industry.

Since the 1970s, computer technology improved both the recording and playing of music. Compact discs and digital audio tape are two ways of listening to accurately reproduced sounds.

*A compact disc plays back sound which has been recorded as a series of digital numbers.*

Microscopic pits that store the digital numbers

# Latin America

Much of Central and South America (also known as Latin America) is enormously rich in agricultural land and minerals. But it has been plagued by unstable or oppressive government and great poverty.

The continent was colonized in the 16th and 17th centuries by the Spanish and Portuguese , but most colonies became independent in the early 19th century.

*An example of colonial architecture in Uruguay*

Since decolonization, military coups or communist revolutions have taken place in almost every country. Many of the regimes have used brutal measures to suppress opposition. Particularly violent were the military dictatorships in Guatemala (from 1954), Chile (1973-1989) and Paraguay (1954-1989).

*The flags of Guatemala, Chile and Paraguay*

Some of these were given economic and military support by the US government, which was anxious to stop communism from spreading in the area. When the Cold War ended, this aid was reduced or withdrawn. In the 1980s, most of these dictatorships were replaced with democratic governments.

## MILITARY DICTATORSHIPS

Brazil and Argentina, the largest countries in Latin America, were ruled by military dictatorships for over 40 years. In Brazil, the army seized power from a democratic government in 1930. Over the next 45 years, the country was ruled by a series of dictatorships, interrupted only by brief periods of democracy. The Brazilian army was brutal in suppressing opposition groups, such as trade unions and human rights organizations.

*Military dictatorships in Latin America*

In the 1930s, the Argentinian economy suffered because of the world depression. The instability which followed was used by the army to seize power. One of the leading army officers was Juan Peron, who ruled the country from 1946 to 1955. With his wife, Eva (known as Evita), he used a direct appeal to the working classes. Despite the restoration of civilian rule in 1955 and his death in 1974, the Peronist party has remained a powerful force in Argentinian politics.

*Eva "Evita" Peron*

During the 1970s, in a period known as the Dirty War, many people were tortured and killed by the army in Argentina. These people are known as the disappeared, because they were arrested without warning and were never seen or heard of again.

*Argentinians holding up photographs of their "disappeared" relatives.*

## THE FALKLANDS WAR

In 1982, Argentina invaded the Falkland Islands, a nearby British colony. Many Argentinians felt that the islands, which they call Las Malvinas, should be part of their territory. British forces were sent out and, after a brief war, the Argentines were expelled. In the face of defeat, the military leader, General Galtieri, resigned and was replaced by a democratic government.

*British ship HMS Sheffield during the Falklands War*

## CUBAN REVOLUTION

In other Latin American countries, such as Mexico, Bolivia, Chile, Nicaragua and Cuba, socialism or communism was seen as a solution to their problems. From the 1930s, Cuba was governed by Gulgencio Batista, a US-backed dictator whose regime was incompetent and corrupt. In 1956, Fidel Castro, a Cuban rebel, joined forces with Che Guevara, an Argentinian Marxist experienced in guerilla warfare.

*This image of Che Guevara became a symbol of revolution all around the world.*

Together they waged a war against Batista and in 1959 they overthrew him. Castro took over government and transformed the Cuban economy. Privately owned sugar and tobacco farms were taken over, and huge reforms in education, public health and transport were introduced. US politicians were worried by events in Cuba as it was so close to their own coastline.

*Fidel Castro*

They soon cut off all economic links between the two countries. In 1959, an unsuccessful invasion of Cuba was carried out by a small band of Cuban exiles trained by the CIA. This failure strengthened Castro's rule. In 1963, Cuba was used as a pawn in the struggle between the USSR and the USA in the Cuban Missile Crisis (see page 46).

## NICARAGUA

From 1933, Nicaragua was ruled by the Somoza family. In the 1960s, nationalists and communists called Sandinistas, used guerilla tactics to get rid of them. Full civil war broke out in 1976 and, after three years of heavy fighting, the Sandinistas took control. They introduced socialist reforms in education, land, housing and health care.

*Sandinista guerilla fighters*

The government had to defend itself from attacks by the US-backed Contras (right-wing Nicaraguans). In 1987, it emerged that US officials had been selling weapons illegally to Iran, and giving the profits from these deals to the Contras. This was called the Irangate scandal. In 1990, the Sandinistas were defeated in a democratic election, and peacefully gave up power.

*Oliver North. He headed the plan to use US arms profits to fund the Contras.*

## JAILED DICTATOR

The US government used its economic strength to influence the political situation in other Latin American countries, including Colombia, El Salvador and Chile.

*Map showing the Panama Canal*

Panama was important to world shipping because of its canal. In the 1980s, it was ruled by General Noriega. He was involved in the illegal drugs trade between Latin America and the USA and also appeared to be selling US military secrets. In 1989, US troops invaded Panama and overthrew him. He was arrested, tried and jailed in the USA for drug-dealing.

## PROBLEMS CONTINUE

Most Latin American economies rely on the export of one or two products, such as sugar or coffee. If the prices of these products become low, the whole economy suffers. This century, the prices of imported goods have risen more than the prices of their exports. As a result, many countries can no longer afford to import vital goods like oil. In the 1970s, most Latin American countries tried to improve their economies by borrowing from foreign banks. By 1980, however, it became clear that they could not pay back the money. This led to what is known as the Debt Crisis.

*A poor district in Brazil*

# China and Japan since 1945

China and Japan followed very different paths in the years following the Second World War. Japan was occupied by US troops from 1945 until 1951, while China remained free of foreign presence.

## CHINA AT HOME

The Japanese withdrawal led to a civil war in China between the communists and nationalists, the *Guomindang*. The communists, led by Mao Zedong, used guerilla warfare to defeat the nationalists.

In October 1949, Mao Zedong proclaimed the establishment of the communist People's Republic of China. The Guomindang fled to the small nearby island of Taiwan, where they founded their own Republic of China.

*The flag of the People's Republic of China*

The large star shows the common goal which unites all the Chinese.

## CHINA ABROAD

The Japanese had controlled Korea since 1910, but after their defeat in 1945, the country was divided into North Korea (occupied by Soviet troops) and South Korea (occupied by US troops). From 1950 to 1953, communist North Korea fought against South Korea in a civil war (see page 48). The communists were aided by China and the USSR, while the South Koreans were supported by the UN. At the end of the war, Korea was permanently divided.

In the late 1950s, the relationship between the two major communist powers, China and the USSR, began to deteriorate. In 1960, China broke the alliance between them, partly because growing Soviet interference in Vietnam threatened Chinese importance in Southeast Asia. During the 1960s, the split became more evident, as China reopened relations with the USA. Membership of the UN followed in 1971.

*US tanks in Korea*

## CULTURAL REVOLUTION

In the early 1950s, Chinese leaders attempted to strengthen control over the country and to restore the economy. In 1953, a Five Year Plan was introduced to raise agricultural and industrial production.

In 1958, Mao introduced a plan for China to industrialize much more rapidly than other countries had done. It was known as the Great Leap Forward. The plan stressed the need for a high production of steel. To support this, small farms were merged into 3000 state properties. But production fell. This led to a terrible famine from which millions died. By the early 1960s, these policies were stopped as it was clear that they had failed.

In 1966, Mao began a plan to revitalize communism, in which all capitalist or western influences were attacked. This is known as the Cultural Revolution. Volunteers travelled the country, carrying a copy of the "Little Red Book" of the *Thoughts of Chairman Mao*. Senior officials were attacked and replaced with Mao's own people. Buildings and schools were closed down and millions were murdered.

After Mao's death in 1976, a set of liberal economic reforms was introduced by the new leader, Deng Ziaoping. In 1979, full diplomatic relations were reopened between China and the USA.

Huge portraits of Mao were held up by supporters of the Cultural Revolution.

Volunteers holding up Mao's book of sayings

*This illustration shows a demonstration held in support of Mao during the Cultural Revolution.*

In 1981, Mao's closest associates (including his widow) were executed as punishment for their part in the Cultural Revolution. By 1982, many aspects of capitalism had been reintroduced in China. This led to an increase in production and export. In 1954, 75% of China's foreign trade had been with communist countries; in 1984 it was less than 10%.

## TIANANMEN MASSACRE

Western attitudes and influences arrived along with consumer goods and capitalism. Young Chinese people began to demand complete democracy. In April 1989, popular pressure for democracy led to a gathering of young, peaceful protesters in Tiananmen Square, Beijing. In early June that year, 300,000 government troops entered Beijing with cars, tanks and guns. They opened fire on the protesters, killing thousands of them. This incident provoked worldwide anger and protest. But the Chinese government did not resign, and many of the previous liberal reforms were reversed.

*19 year-old Wang Weilin stood in front of army tanks, forcing them to halt.*

# JAPAN

From 1945 to 1951, Japan was occupied by the victorious Allies of the Second World War. Douglas MacArthur, the US general in charge of the occupation, ordered a new constitution which gave women the vote and workers the right to form unions. Emperor Hirohito accepted a reduction in his powers. After the foundation of a communist republic in China, the US government tried to help rebuild the Japanese economy, to make Japan strong against communism. Japan was not allowed to make weapons, and it was not until 1992 that it was allowed to send troops to other countries.

Japan suffered greatly in the Second World War. Over two million Japanese had been killed, its road and rail systems were badly damaged and many industries and cities were destroyed. But, in some ways, the effects of war helped Japan's economy to boom.

During the war, many engineers and scientists had been trained and mechanization had been increased. After the war, these skills could no longer be directed at building arms, so other industries had to be developed instead. New educational reforms emphasized the teaching of science and technology at school.

During the 1950s, economic development became a source of national pride. In 1966, Japan began generating its own nuclear power. By 1968, average

*Japan's weapons, like this one, were funded by the USA.*

incomes had tripled since the war and Japan's economy was greater than that of West Germany.

*The Japanese flag, known as "the Rising Sun"*

Since 1974, Japan has developed many industries abroad. Japanese companies have been able take advantage of other countries' supplies of raw materials and cheaper land and salaries. They also avoid paying a tariff on exported goods if they are sold in the countries in which they are manufactured. The countries in competition with Japan have criticized its trade surplus and domination of industry. Japan has reacted to these criticisms by becoming the world's largest donor of foreign aid and by increasing its tourism. Other countries, having encouraged Japanese economic recovery, often resent the success that Japan has achieved in making and selling technical goods.

*A Japanese personal stereo*

# Media and communications

D ramatic developments in media and communications in the course of the century have had enormous effects on people's lives. In 1900, there were no radios, televisions or public telephone networks. The introduction of all these, along with faster travel, has led to a "mass society", in which people over a wide area share tastes and opinions. Mass production has meant that new inventions are cheaper and available to more people than ever before.

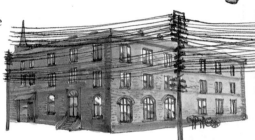

*Telegraph wires criss-crossed streets in 1900.*

## NEW WAVES

The existence of radio waves was first demonstrated in 1888, by the German scientist Heinrich Hertz. By 1901, the Italian Guglielmo Marconi had invented equipment for transmitting radio waves across the Atlantic (from Britain to Canada) by using an antenna raised by a kite. Radios were used to send messages and to direct air traffic during the First World War.

In the 1920s, public broadcasting systems were set up in Europe and the USA, used for information and entertainment. Governments then used radios to broadcast propaganda against the enemy during the Second World War.

*An early plastic radio*

During the Cold War, both the USSR and the USA sent political messages over the airwaves. A US radio station called Radio Free Europe was set up to transmit news of the West and democratic life to people living in communist countries in the Eastern bloc.

*Marconi with his early transatlantic radio*

## TELEPHONES

The first telephone was invented by Alexander Graham Bell in 1876. Using radio technology, transatlantic telephone links between London and New York were opened in 1926. This was not a practical system though, because only one call could be made at a time.

*This is a 1905 "candlestick" telephone. All calls were made through a central exchange by lifting the earpiece.*

Mouthpiece

Earpiece

*An early experimental telephone made by Bell in 1875*

*A 1930s plastic 'phone. Local calls could be made directly.*

Mouthpiece

Earpiece

Handset lifted to activate 'phone.

To make a call, the numbers on the dial were turned clockwise.

*A modern cordless 'phone*

Push button numbers

Last number repeat button to redial your last call.

A more efficient system was introduced in 1956, when undersea cables were laid to relay overseas telephone calls. But it was still very expensive to 'phone abroad. This only became possible after the invention of the microchip and advances in space technology in the 1970s. Calls from around the world could be relayed by a satellite in space, without having to be connnected by an operator.

*An optical fibre cable*

## MOVING PICTURES

At the end of the 19th century, the first movie projectors were introduced by Thomas Edison in the USA, and by the Lumière brothers in France. They showed a series of photographs in a quick sequence, so that they appeared to show continuous action. These "silent" films soon became an extremely popular form of entertainment. Cinemas could entertain many more people at once, than actors could by performing in a single theatre. As a result, silent film actors, like Charlie Chaplin and Mary Pickford, became famous and very rich.

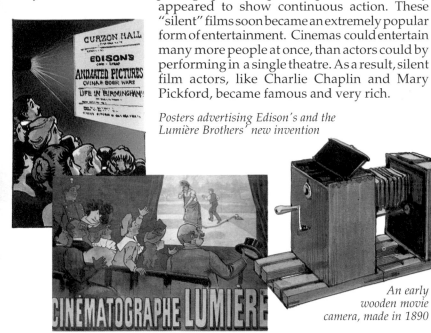

*Posters advertising Edison's and the Lumière Brothers' new invention*

*An early wooden movie camera, made in 1890*

*The Jazz Singer* is usually considered to be the first talking picture, even though the film only contained a couple of songs and small sections of dialogue. Many people believed that "talkies" would never catch on, but by 1930 they had almost completely replaced silent films.

Governments and political groups recognized the propaganda value of films, and soon began to use them to communicate their ideas.

*Posters for the first talking film "The Jazz Singer" and the revolutionary Soviet film "Battleship Potemkin"*

WARNER BROS. SUPREME TRIUMPH
**AL JOLSON** IN "the **JAZZ SINGER**"

With the growth of television networks in the 1950s, cinema became less and less popular. So producers invented new ways to try to persuade audiences to go to the cinema. "Cinemascope" was a technique by which the screen was made much wider, so that the film appeared to surround the audience. Another innovation introduced at the same time was three-dimensional, or 3-D, film. By wearing special cardboard spectacles with one green and one red plastic lens, the audience could see images that seemed to come out from the screen right at them. But neither of these techniques could compete successfully with the new medium of television.

*People watching a 3-D film with their special glasses*

## TELEVISION

The first television system was demonstrated in the 1920s in Britain by John Logie Baird. The picture consisted of a series of moving black and white shapes. In 1936, the first television service for the public began in Britain.

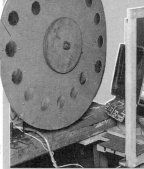

*John Logie Baird and the early television*

After the Second World War, television became the most popular form of entertainment, as more people could afford to own a set. In developed countries, several different channels were established.

*Small television, with 55mm (2.2 inch) screen*

The first live satellite broadcast was in 1962 (see page 63). This allowed television images being filmed in the USA to be shown at the same time in Europe. Satellites have made events immediately available to an international audience. Today, people can see, read and listen to the news, almost as it happens.

*A European communications satellite suspended in space*

Solar panels to absorb power from the Sun

# The microchip revolution

The most important invention of the second half of the 20th century is the microchip (or silicon chip). Today, there are very few areas of life that are unaffected by the design and use of microchips. Because of this, people talk of an "electronic revolution" in the same way that they would talk of the industrial revolution in the 18th and 19th centuries.

*Credit cards like this have a built-in computer which records each payment.*

## CHIPS WITH EVERYTHING

Microelectronic technology has advanced in stages. The first stage was the valve, an electronic device which increased electric signals and acted as an on-off switch. In 1947, US scientists invented the transistor. It was similar to a valve, but smaller, faster and cheaper.

In 1957, the world's first microchip was invented. This was a whole electronic circuit concentrated onto a tiny wafer of silicon, an element obtained from sand. Soon electrical circuitry which would have filled a whole room before could fit onto a chip smaller than a pinhead.

*A valve and a transistor*

*A silicon chip is smaller than an insect.*

## COMPUTERS

The most outstanding use of the microchip has been in computers, machines which store and process information. In 1946, one of the first electronic computers ENIAC (Electronic Numerical Integrator and Calculator) was switched on in the USA. It only held 20 numbers

*ENIAC, the world's first electronic computer*

Wires had to be changed to make a new calculation.

ENIAC covered 74 sq m (8000 sq feet) of floor space.

Trained computer operator

Almost 2000 valves added to ENIAC's bulk.

ENIAC weighed the same as 500 people.

*This small desk-top computer stores much more information than the whole of ENIAC.*

and the whole system had to be re-wired to change its program.

In the 1950s, computers containing transistors were built. Although more advanced than ENIAC, these new computers were still expensive and only used by governments, scientists and a few businesses. But once computers could be made with silicon chips, banks and small businesses were able to afford them.

*A modern computer game*

The age of mass computer ownership began in the mid 1970s, when microcomputers using very small efficient chips were introduced. Soon computers became an essential part of modern life. Many people now have home computers, while most businesses use them for word processing and accounts. Computers also play an important role in space travel, hospitals, government and warfare.

## CHIP COMMUNICATIONS

Most of the advances in space technology have depended on the development of the microchip. In 1957, Soviet space engineers launched the first artificial satellite, an unmanned spacecraft which orbited the Earth. Since then, satellites have transformed the world's communications.

*This is a balloon satellite, which was used to bounce off radio signals in space.*

In 1960, the USA put the *Echo* and *Courier* satellites into orbit and relayed the first satellite telephone calls between the USA and Europe. Before this, calls across the Atlantic were transmitted by underwater telephone cable. Two years later, the *Telstar* satellite transmitted the first live transatlantic television broadcast from the USA to Europe.

*The satellite Telstar 1 broadcasting the first live transatlantic link-up*

The speech was filmed and relayed up.

The image was received and broadcast by ground stations in France and the UK.

Telstar weighed 77kg (170lb) and was covered with 360 solar cells.

Within a quarter of a century, there were several thousand satellites orbiting the Earth. Satellites have improved the accuracy of weather forecasting, by transmitting photographs which show cloud and wind formations.

*This satellite photo shows cloud patterns over Britain and France.*

# FAX FACTS

A facsimile or fax machine is one which can send documents through telephone lines in less than a minute. A very early version was thought to have been invented in the 19th century, but the modern fax machine was not refined and widely produced until the late 1980s. First there was the telex machine, which could only send computer type. Later the technology improved and images could be sent as well as words.

*A 1990s fax machine*

At the sending end, a document is fed into the fax machine.

Light bounces off the paper, reflecting the face of the document onto a lens.

The image is broken down into a series of black and white dots, and a series of tiny horizontal lines.

All this information is sent down the telephone lines.

On the receiving fax, the telephone signals are converted back into dots and lines.

These dots and lines remake the original image sent, anywhere in the world.

# ROBOTS AND ROBOTICS

In the second half of the century, advances in computers provided the technology needed to develop robots, machines which carry out tasks automatically. Industrial robots, usually computer-controlled mechanical arms, were introduced into factories in the developed world to perfom simple repetitive tasks. Robots have proved to be particularly useful on production lines and in nuclear power stations. Computer-controlled arms can repair the parts of a reactor that are dangerous for people to enter.

*A robotic arm used to weld metal in a factory*

Water and air system

Water and air supply hoses

Mains power supply

Power source for motors

Flexible "elbow" joint of robotic arm

Welding gun

*A home robot, used to perform very basic tasks*

# Space exploration

Technology developed during the Second World War made space exploration a practical possibility for the first time. In 1942, the Germans launched the V-2 (see page 31). This was the first long-distance rocket and the ancestor of almost all space rockets.

During the Cold War, the political rivalry between the superpowers encouraged them to develop their own space projects. They turned to rockets as a means of sending atomic weapons over a long range. This in turn led to more research into space travel.

## DOGS IN SPACE

During the 1950s, both the USA and the USSR developed the technology to build unmanned spacecraft, called satellites, which could orbit the Earth. In October 1957, the Russians launched the satellite *Sputnik 1*, the first vehicle to go into space. Only a month later, *Sputnik 2* was launched. It contained a dog named Laika, the first live animal to be sent out into space.

By 1990, there were hundreds of satellites in orbit, relaying weather information, telephone calls and television pictures (see pages 63). Once in orbit, these satellites can float in space forever.

*This picture shows the rocket which propelled Sputnik 2 into space.*

## PEOPLE IN SPACE

In 1961, the Soviet Union launched the first person into space. The Soviet cosmonaut, Yuri Gagarin, completed a whole orbit of the Earth in the craft *Vostok 1* in 108 minutes. On his return to Earth, he became one of the USSR's greatest heroes. Less than a month later, the Americans sent out their first astronaut, Alan Shepard, but his flight only lasted 15 minutes and did not orbit the Earth. The US rocket launcher was far smaller than the Russian one.

*Gagarin's descent procedure*

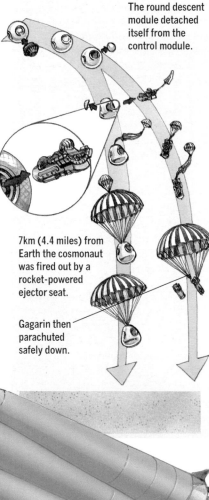

The round descent module detached itself from the control module.

7km (4.4 miles) from Earth the cosmonaut was fired out by a rocket-powered ejector seat.

Gagarin then parachuted safely down.

*In 1965, Alexei Leonov (USSR) was the first person to "walk in space". He floated for about 20 minutes.*

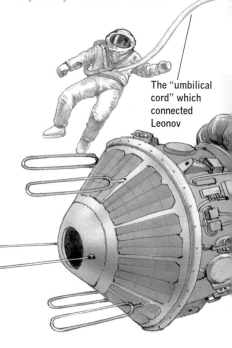

The "umbilical cord" which connected Leonov

## MOON LANDINGS

In the early 1960s, the Soviets were winning the space race. The US space department, NASA, wanted to change this and so in 1961, announced their intention of landing astronauts on the Moon. NASA sent out a number of unmanned vehicles, called space probes, to collect information and test new technology. In 1966, the Soviet probe *Luna 9* landed on the Moon and took samples of soil and photographs. Before this landing it had been thought that the surface of the Moon might be covered with a thick dust.

Sputnik 2 was inside this protective cone.

Launch vehicle rocket boosters

Laika, the first animal in space

Television cameras to film Leonov

Airlock cabin through which Leonov left from the craft

The pilot of the spacecraft, Pavel Belyayev

## SPACE SHUTTLES

As the rockets used to propel the craft upward to the Moon had no way of landing safely, they could not be used again. Rockets were abandoned to float forever in space. This made space exploration very expensive. But in the 1970s, NASA developed a reusable spacecraft called a space shuttle, which was able to land like a conventional plane. The first space shuttle to go into orbit was the *Columbia*, launched in 1981. It had comfortable quarters for a crew of seven and made several flights. There was a series of successful shuttle launches until 1986, when the US shuttle *Challenger* exploded shortly after launch, due to a fault in one of the booster rockets. All work on the shuttles was then suspended.

## OTHER PLANETS

*This picture of Saturn and its moons was taken by a Voyager probe.*

Space exploration has led to the gathering of information about other planets. Throughout the 1970s, unmanned space probes from the USSR and USA were sent to Mercury, Venus and Mars. Data about these planets was relayed back to Earth. More recently, the US probes *Voyagers 1* and *2* have taken clear photographs of Jupiter, Saturn, Uranus and Neptune, the planets farthest from Earth in the solar system.

## COSMOLOGY

Cosmology is the study of the universe. During the 1920s, the American astronomer Edwin Hubble showed that there are many other galaxies, which are moving away from our own. From these findings came the "Big Bang" theory, which suggests that the universe originated in one enormous explosion.

Revised versions of the theory have been put forward by several scientists, including Stephen Hawking and Roger Penrose. Part of their research on the universe after the Big Bang focuses on the fundamental types of force in nature. One of the main aims of modern science is to use these astronomical observations to build up a complete unified theory, explaining the way that the universe and the planets behave.

Scientists suspected the dust might be so deep that it would swallow up a whole spacecraft. *Luna 9* proved that the surface was solid.

On July 16, 1969, NASA launched the spacecraft *Apollo 11*. Once in space, the detachable landing module separated from the control module and landed on an area of the Moon known as the Sea of Tranquillity. The two astronauts, Neil Armstrong and Edwin Aldrin, spent about two and a half hours on the Moon. Between 1969 and 1972, there were five US Moon landings, which are thought to have cost a total of about $25 billion.

*An American space shuttle and its rocket launcher*

Shuttle

*The astronaut, Edwin Aldrin, standing on the Moon*

Launcher

Booster rocket

*After 1945, radio telescopes with large dish reflectors were introduced to improve the study of other planets.*

# The European Community

The European Community grew out of a desire for peace and unity after the dislocation of two world wars. After 1945, Europe divided into two camps: the Eastern bloc (dominated by the communist USSR) and the Western bloc (allied to the USA). Over the next 50 years, many Western European governments strengthened economic and political links and progressed toward a united Europe.

War had left the continent weak, both physically and economically. To boost the recovery and protect Europe from communism, the USA gave massive financial handouts (of over $13 billion) to Western Europe in a scheme called the Marshall Plan.

Many believed that political and economic stability could only be achieved by greater unity. The Council of Europe was formed in 1949 with this aim. It hoped to preserve freedom, democracy and the rule of law. European unity was also seen as a way of helping to prevent domination by either the USA or the USSR.

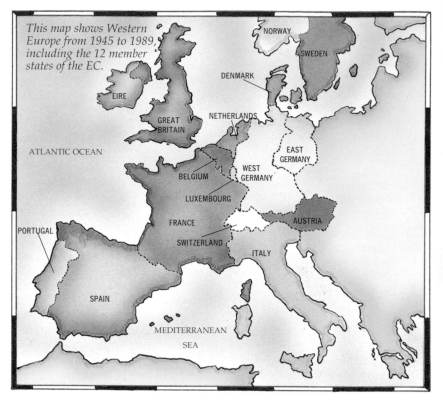

*This map shows Western Europe from 1945 to 1989, including the 12 member states of the EC.*

## EARLY ECONOMIC UNIONS

Germany and France had fought each other three times in 70 years. The French foreign minister, Robert Schuman, believed that the best way to prevent war was to unite their steel and coal industries, making it impossible for either country to make weapons secretly.

*A coal mine in Germany*

At the same time, the efficiency of these industries would be improved. In 1950, the European Coal and Steel Community (ECSC) was formed. France and Germany were joined by Italy, Belgium, the Netherlands and Luxembourg.

In 1957, two more unions were founded: the European Atomic Energy Commission (Euratom), dealing with nuclear research and energy, and the European Economic Commission (the EEC), also known as the Common Market. The aim of the EEC was to improve Europe's economic position by creating common policies. Its original members were those of the ECSC. Britain tried to join in 1961, but entry was twice blocked by the French president, Charles de Gaulle. In 1973,

*Charles de Gaulle*

membership was granted to Britain, Denmark and Eire. Spain, Greece, and Portugal joined in the 1980s, making a total of 12 members.

The EEC developed common policies for agriculture, trade and immigration and dropped trade barriers between EEC countries. The Common Agricultural Policy (CAP) stabilized food prices and increased agricultural production by giving money to European farmers. CAP, however, has proved very expensive. By the 1980s, it was using 60% of the EEC budget, which has caused disagreements between the member states.

*CAP has led to surplus "mountains" of grain.*

# THE EUROPEAN COMMUNITY

In 1967, the ECSC, Euratom and the EEC merged into one institution, known as the European Community (the EC). This has grown into a wide-ranging body which plays a major role in European affairs. It has four key institutions: the Commission, the Court of Justice, the Council of Ministers and the Parliament.

The Council of Ministers, which generally meets in Belgium, is made up of nominated ministers from the governments of each of the member states. This is the main decision-making body of the EC.

*The EC Commission Building in Belgium*

The European Court of Justice in Luxembourg is a legal institution, where 13 judges from the states decide on private and public disputes that arise from EC treaties or laws.

*The Court of Justice in Luxembourg*

*MEPs in full session in Strasbourg, with each block representing a different political group.*

*The EC flag*

In 1976, the European Council, part of the Council of Ministers, was set up as the meeting place for the presidents and prime ministers of the member states. The Council discusses general and foreign policy.

Every five years, the people of the member states elect 518 representatives to the European Parliament. Members of Parliament (MEPs) debate the proposals of the Commission and suggest changes. The number of MEPs from each country depends on population.

*The 1993 Commission*

The Commission, based in Belgium, proposes laws and puts new policies into practice. It is led by 17 people, each nominated by the governments of the 12 member states.

## NEW EC MEMBERS

In 1989 and 1990, the ruling communist parties of Eastern Europe collapsed and were replaced by new governments (see pages 68-71). This has raised new questions about membership of the Community. Many of the former communist states wish to join the EC, but they are much poorer than existing member countries. Other, richer countries, such as Sweden, Finland and Austria, also want to join, as well as poorer ones such as Turkey, Malta and Cyprus. There is uncertainty in the EC about which should be allowed to join first.

## THE EC AT THE END OF THE CENTURY

Recently, there have been debates about extending the powers of the EC and making Europe more united. Some members want a single European market and a European federation (a larger political unit created from previously smaller, separate ones). Some want a "United States of Europe" to work in the same way as the United States of America.

The states vary in their commitment to European federation. Britain and Denmark are cautious, while Germany and Italy are pressing to go forward. A united European foreign policy and a single currency (called ECU) have been proposed. In the future, there might also be a police force and an army. Since the unification of Germany, the EC represents about 340 million people, which makes it bigger than the USA. Some people are worried about the power and size of the newly united Germany, but many are optimistic that the EC will continue to help Europe to avoid war and promote economic stability.

*An ECU coin*

# The breakdown of communism

For over 40 years, the Soviet government in Moscow dominated 23 million sq km (9 million square miles) of territory stretching across Europe and Asia. During the 1980s, the Eastern bloc began to crumble. At the end of the decade, a wave of reforms and democratic revolutions led to the dramatic breakdown of the entire Soviet system.

## MIKHAIL GORBACHEV

Many changes were a product of the reforms of Mikhail Gorbachev, who became leader of the USSR in 1985. He inherited an ethnically mixed country with many political, social and economic problems.

Gorbachev launched a plan of reform known as *perestroika,* (meaning "restructuring"). He wanted to make the USSR more efficient. To do this he needed the people's support and so he encouraged greater openness, in a policy known as *glasnost.* Newspapers and television stations began revealing many of the horrors of the past, and many political prisoners were released. Journalists then began to examine current economic and social problems. Gorbachev also believed that Eastern Europe should be given more independence.

*Mikhail Gorbachev*

## GORBACHEV ABROAD

The USSR could no longer afford to compete with the USA in the production of nuclear arms, especially since the US president, Ronald Reagan, had increased military spending. Gorbachev therefore felt it was vital to bring a speedy end to the Cold War.

In May 1988, all the Soviet troops were pulled out of Afghanistan, after almost ten years of involvement there. Later that year, both superpowers agreed to reduce their nuclear arms capacities in an agreement called the INF Treaty.

*1987 Soviet peace poster*

## LAST DAYS

In 1988, the Communist Party gave Gorbachev greater power. In March 1989, he used these powers to hold free elections for a congress of deputies. Some leading communists were defeated by radical reformers such as Boris Yeltsin, a former ally of Gorbachev's, who became the representative for Moscow. All over the USSR, nationalist groups were gaining support, especially in the Caucasus and the Baltic states.

## SOLIDARITY IN POLAND

There were two opposition groups in Poland: trade unions and the Catholic Church. *Solidarnosc* (meaning "Solidarity"), a trade union which was not part of the Communist Party, was formed in 1980. Under the leadership of Lech Walesa, it organized protests and strikes. The government then banned it and declared martial law. But trade unions continued to demand reforms.

In the summer of 1988, strikes spread through the country. The government was then forced to talk to Solidarity. At meetings held in the spring of 1989, it was agreed that Solidarity and the communists should share power until free elections were held.

*Lech Walesa in 1980*

*The Solidarity banner*

In these elections, the first democratic ones for over 40 years, Solidarity won an overwhelming victory. Tadeusz Mazowiecki was appointed the first non-communist prime minister in the Soviet bloc. In 1990, Lech Walesa was elected President of Poland. Gorbachev and the USSR did nothing to stop these developments.

## HUNGARY FOR CHANGE

The Communist Party of Hungary had been introducing capitalist policies since the mid-1970s, but Gorbachev's reforms led to even greater change. In 1988, a new government formed in Hungary, with younger, more liberal leaders.

In May 1989, the barbed wire fences between Hungary and Austria were removed. Other parties formed and free elections were held in March 1990. The non-communist group Democratic Forum won the most votes and its leader, Josef Antall, was asked to form a government.

## TUMBLING WALLS

Although East Germany (the GDR) was one of the wealthier countries in the Eastern bloc, economic conditions were poor compared with those in West Germany. This led to anti-Soviet feeling within the GDR. Many East Germans risked being shot by trying to escape to the West over the Berlin Wall.

Despite anti-Soviet feeling, Erich Honecker, the president since 1971, refused to reform. His party, the SED, followed a strict Stalinist policy. But the opening up of the border between Hungary and Austria gave East Germans an alternative way out of the GDR. In 1989, 20,000 people took to the streets in Leipzig, to demand that opposition parties be allowed. Leipzig's Church of St Nicholas became a national focus for pro-democracy groups.

*The grave of a German shot at the Berlin Wall*

Further demonstrations broke out in early October, when Gorbachev visited the GDR and criticized the SED. The government's obvious lack of popularity led to Honecker's resignation on October 18. His successor, Egon Krenz, agreed to hold free elections and, on November 9, he gave orders for the Berlin Wall to be demolished. Thousands of German people celebrated as they were reunited with family and friends in the opposite sector.

In March 1990, the first free elections were won by the Christian Democrat party. They then began talks with West Germany, which resulted in unification on October 23, 1990.

*The demolition of the Berlin Wall*

People stood on the wall, celebrating the end of the division of Germany.

The west side was covered in graffiti, much of it anti-communist.

People grabbed chunks of the wall to keep as souvenirs.

Water cannons were used to stop people from demolishing the wall in the East.

# The end of the Soviet Union

Encouraged by the events in Poland, Hungary and East Germany, the remaining countries in the Eastern bloc overthrew their communist rulers. On New Year's Eve 1991 came the final collapse of the USSR itself.

## THE VELVET REVOLUTION

After the failure of the 1968 reforms (see page 49), Czech politicians followed a hardline communist policy. But resistance to the regime grew. In 1977, a human rights organization called Charter 77 was formed, led by the playwright, Vaclav Havel.

In 1988, the prime minister, Ladislav Adamec, introduced some reforms, but many Czechoslovakians wanted to end communism completely. Inspired by events in Germany, young people led a pro-democracy demonstration in Prague on November 17. Although it was peaceful, the riot police attacked many protesters. On November 20, over 200,000 people gathered in Prague's Wenceslas Square, and protests quickly spread. Opposition

*The statue of St. Wenceslas, in Prague's main square, became a meeting place for reformers.*

groups formed in the country's two main regions: Civic Forum in Prague (capital of the Czech lands) and Public Against Violence in Bratislava (the capital of the Slovakian area of the country). The government was forced to resign on November 27, following some demonstrations and a two hour general strike. A month later, Vaclav Havel was elected president by a coalition of politicians. Free elections were held the following June. These events are known as the Velvet Revolution, because they were mostly non-violent.

*Vaclav Havel*

Songs and speeches were delivered from the statue.

Peace sign painted like a Czech flag

Pro-democracy poster

Poster of Dubček, the leader of the 1968 revolution

Civic Forum logo

## BULGARIA

The "revolution" in Bulgaria came as a reaction from the communist party itself to events in other Eastern bloc states. In 1989, the communist leader Zhikov was replaced by Mladenov, who promised to introduce democracy. By the end of the year, the communist party had agreed to end its monopoly and to allow democratic elections.

## ROMANIA

Since 1965, Romania had been governed by President Ceausescu. He was a harsh leader, who often destroyed villages to force people to move to industrial areas. He was especially ruthless against the Hungarian minority living in Romania.

In December 1989, protests began in Timisoara, a town with a mostly Hungarian population. The state security force, the *Securitate*, fired on protesters. News of this spread unrest throughout Romania.

On December 21, 1989, Ceausescu addressed a crowd in the capital, Bucharest, but they shouted him down. The people, joined by the army, overpowered the Securitate, and the president was arrested. On Christmas day, Ceausescu and his wife were put on trial, found guilty and executed. Fighting died down and free elections were held in May. The NSF, a coalition of ex-communists and communists, won the elections and formed a government. The NSF leader, Ilescu, became president.

*Romanian troops fighting on the streets of Bucharest*

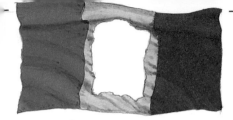

*People waved the Romanian flag with the communist symbol ripped from the middle.*

## BACK IN THE USSR

Nationalists in the Baltic states of Latvia, Estonia and Lithuania were inspired by events in Eastern Europe. In 1990, Lithuania declared its independence. Gorbachev did not want the USSR to break up entirely and reacted by introducing an economic blockade. But the Baltic states continued to fight for independence. In January 1991, Soviet forces entered Latvia and Lithuania and attempted to stop these developments by taking over parliament and the media.

## SOVIET COUP D'ETAT

After the events in the Baltic states, prospects for further reform in the USSR looked doubtful. Politicians and army leaders were divided between hardliners, who wanted to maintain the union of the republics of the USSR, and reformers, who wanted each republic to be more independent. Gorbachev was criticized by both sides. Things were made more difficult for him when Boris Yeltsin, his main rival for power, was elected president of the Russian Republic. More power to the republics would also mean more power for Yeltsin.

Gorbachev's final act as leader was to negotiate the New Union Treaty, which proposed to make each republic more independent. It was due to be signed on August 20, 1991, but the hardliners wanted to stop the treaty from going through. They seized power in a *coup d'état* while Gorbachev was away from the capital, and formed a committee under the leadership of five men, including the heads of the KGB and the armed forces. The committee ordered that all media offices be closed down. Troops and tanks took up positions in the streets of Moscow and Leningrad and Gorbachev was made a prisoner in his own home.

Reformers looked to Yeltsin for action. He made a rousing speech from the streets calling for firm resistance. Many people came out to show their support and the troops seemed unwilling to use force to disperse them. Faced with this opposition, the leaders of the coup resigned. Within two hours, Yeltsin had taken over full command of the armed forces.

*Boris Yeltsin*

## DEATH OF THE USSR

Gorbachev returned to Moscow, but Yeltsin was the new hero of democracy. In the central Russian parliament, Gorbachev and Yeltsin battled for leadership. Yeltsin pushed for the break-up of the Soviet Union, and with it 70 years of communism. He proved to be the stronger of the two. At midnight on December 31, 1991, the USSR ceased to exist. Gorbachev, as President of the Union, was out of a job. The Russian Federal Republic became a separate state, with Yeltsin as president, while the other republics became independent.

*This map shows the USSR after 1991.*

The Russian Federation

Estonia
Latvia
Lithuania
Belarussia
Ukraine
Azerbaijan
Georgia
Moldova   BLACK SEA
Armenia

*Days after the coup was crushed, crowds gathered to destroy symbols of communism, like this statue of Dzerzhinsky, founder of the Soviet secret police.*

*The old Soviet flag was taken down and replaced with the traditional Russian flag.*

# The Middle East

At the beginning of the 20th century, vast oil supplies were discovered in the Middle East. Today Iran, Iraq, Saudi Arabia and the Gulf States are the world's main oil-producing nations. The importance of oil for industry and transport has ensured that the area has a crucial position in inter-national affairs. But the political situation has been complicated by religious tensions in the area, between Muslims and Jews and between the two Muslim sects: the Sunnis and the Shias.

*Map of the Middle East*

## STRIKING OIL

The exploitation of oil began in 1902, with British companies drilling oil in Iran. The oil wells of Iraq, Kuwait and Saudi Arabia were not opened up until after 1945.

At first, control of the oil wells was in the hands of US, British and French companies. But, in 1959, OPEC (the Organization of Petroleum Exporting Countries) was formed to increase the power of the oil producers in relation to foreign oil companies. OPEC raised oil prices and cut oil production after the Yom Kippur War (see page 43). This was an attempt to force western countries into changing their pro-Israeli policies. As less oil was sold, prices rose quickly, making Arab and other producers very rich. Western politicians tried to reduce their complete reliance on Middle Eastern oil, by looking for new oil supplies and cutting down on their fuel consumption.

*An oil well*

## REVOLUTION IN IRAN

Between 1925 and 1979, Iran, a Shia Muslim nation, was ruled by the Pahlavi dynasty. The ruler was called the Shah, meaning "King of kings". In the 1940s, Shah Mohammed Reza introduced influences from the West to try to modernize Iran. He was over-thrown in 1953 by Muslims who resented foreign influence, but was restored with US and British aid. He then established a dictatorship and launched his "white revolution", consisting of land and economic reforms. Many Iranians opposed the government's reforms, especially in 1973, when a rise in oil prices led to inflation and social upheaval. Opposition to the Shah was ruthlessly suppressed by his secret police, *Savak*.

Devout Shias looked to an Islamic holy man, Ayatollah Khomeini, to lead them. He had been exiled since 1964 for his political activities, but while abroad continued to produce propaganda criticizing the Shah.

Shiite revolts broke out in 1978 and went on for 12 months. The army killed many protesters, but the government was unable to keep control. The Shah fled the country and Khomeini returned to take control. Iran became a republic led

*Islamic women mourning the Ayatollah at his funeral in 1989*

by extreme Muslims known as Islamic fundamentalists. Half a million people, mainly from the middle classes, fled the country, while thousands of those who remained were executed for being "enemies of the revolution".

## THE HOSTAGE CRISIS

Khomeini encouraged Iranians to hate the West, especially the USA. In 1979, Iranian students seized the US Embassy and held its staff hostage for 444 days. They demanded that US politicians send the Shah back to Iran. The USA refused, freezing $11 billion of Iranian assets and banning imports of Iranian oil.

The crisis ended in January 1981. The hostages were freed and the US government promised not to interfere in Iranian affairs.

## IRAN AND IRAQ

*Iran's flag (top) and Iraq's flag*

In 1980, war broke out between Iran and Iraq, as a result of a long-running border dispute. The chaos in Iran caused by the revolution gave the Iraqi leader, Saddam Hussein, the chance to invade. The Iraqis advanced into Iran, but were pushed back by the Iranians.

For the next seven years, Iraq defended itself from annual Iranian attacks. The Iraqis used poison gas in the conflict and both sides bombed civilians and tried to destroy the other's oil industries. Iran lost 600,000 lives and Iraq around 150,000. In 1988, a UN ceasefire took effect and pre-war borders were restored.

## SADDAM HUSSEIN

The Iraqi leader, Saddam Hussein, had taken part in a political murder by the time he was only 16 years old. In the 1950s, he became an assassin for the Ba'ath party, which aimed to establish a single Muslim state across the Arab world. The party came to power in Iraq in 1968. Hussein became vice president and then leader, using violence against his enemies and expanding the army.

*Saddam Hussein*

## INVASION OF KUWAIT

In the last century, Iraq and Kuwait were ruled jointly by the Ottoman Turks. The two states were first established as separate countries by the British government in 1899. But many Iraqis continued to believe that the two territories should be united. Kuwait, although smaller, was rich in oil.

In August 1990, Iraqi troops invaded and occupied Kuwait. This led to worldwide protest and an immediate rise in oil prices.

*Light amplifying goggles were used in night attacks.*

In an operation codenamed "Desert Shield", 30 countries sent forces to Saudi Arabia to protect oil supplies. The UN declared that if Iraq did not withdraw from Kuwait by January 15, 1991, force could be used. Hussein tried to attract support from other Arab states by exploiting anti-Israeli feeling. He promised that, if a war began, he would attack Israel and win it back for the Arabs.

When Iraq failed to withdraw its forces, the UN ordered an attack codenamed "Desert Storm".

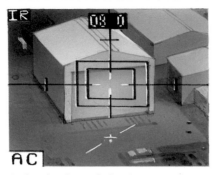

*A plane's photo of a bomb target*

The UN allies launched a heavy six-week air campaign, disrupting life in Iraq. This was followed by a ground invasion of Kuwait, which was liberated in just 100 hours.

During the war, Iraq launched missiles into Israel. But, as Israel did not retaliate, Egypt and Syria remained in the alliance against Iraq. On February 28, a ceasefire was agreed and Iraq gave up claims to Kuwait. The UN banned Iraq from having nuclear, chemical or biological weapons.

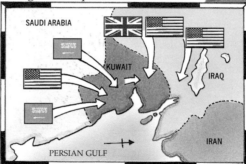

*This map shows operation "Desert Storm" and the protection of Kuwait.*

After the war, two unsuccessful revolts took place inside Iraq, by the Kurds in the north and the Shias in the south. But, despite defeat in the war and unrest at home, Hussein stayed in power.

## OIL DISASTER

The war led to the most serious oil pollution disaster in history, as two million barrels of Kuwaiti oil were deliberately leaked into the Persian Gulf by Iraqi forces. This created huge oil slicks, which killed many species of the local wildlife.

*A seagull suffering the ill effects of the oil spill*

In addition to this, 500 oil wells were set on fire by Iraqi troops. The fires were very difficult to put out and many burned for up to a year. This contributed to environmental damage such as global warming.

*Burning Kuwaiti oil wells*

## THE KURDISH REFUGEES

When the Kurdish revolt failed, Saddam Hussein stepped up a campaign of persecution against them. This created an enormous refugee problem, as hundreds of thousands of Kurds fled to the mountains on the Turkish border, to avoid death at the hands of the Iraqi government.

*Kurdish people, homeless in the mountains of north Iraq*

# Popular protest groups

Throughout this century, various groups have used protest as a way of putting pressure on governments to make changes to laws and policies. Pressure groups apply a range of tactics to draw attention to their aims, from demonstrations and marches, to campaigns of civil disobedience (peaceful refusal to obey the laws of the land).

*This banner was used by French students protesting about government policy in 1968.*

## PEACE MOVEMENTS

Before the end of the 18th century, wars had been fought by small professional armies. But gradually armies grew in size and war began to involve more of the population - civilian as well as miltary.

The roots of the peace movement go back over a hundred years. Its popularity in Europe increased after the enormous loss of life in the First World War.

*This was the emblem for the London Peace Society in 1900.*

The peace movement gained support with its campaign for a League of Nations, at which governments would be forced to discuss problems together. It grew in popularity during the 1930s, as many pledged never to fight again. But others believed that Hitler's aggression made war inevitable. Later, the development of nuclear arms and the Cold War led many people to worry about the prospect of a war. Anti-nuclear groups were formed, like CND (the Campaign for Nuclear Disarmament) in Britain. Europeans felt most at risk from rivalry between the superpowers.

*This is the symbol of the British group CND.*

In the 1950s, marches were held all over the continent. Under the leadership of Albert Einstein, scientists gathered annually to discuss the moral consequences of their inventions. Although it was their work that had made nuclear arms possible in the first place, many argued that the weapons should be abandoned.

After a period of detente, tensions flared up again in the 1980s. The peace movement became more popular than ever, especially in Western Europe. The European Nuclear Disarmament Movement (END) was founded in 1980, as NATO and the Warsaw Pact prepared to install even more powerful and accurate weapons in Europe. Anti-nuclear demonstrations broke out all over the continent. In the USA, the Freeze movement, which aimed to freeze the levels of nuclear arms production, attracted support.

By the end of the Cold War, the peace movement was losing appeal. Many felt that nuclear war was a remote threat. But the movement had succeeded in raising awareness of the risks of war.

*French and US posters protesting against US involvement in the Vietnam War*

*US Pershing missile*

*A European peace rally*

## RIGHTS FOR WOMEN

Feminism, the belief in the social, economic and political equality of women and men, has had a huge impact on the modern world.

At the beginning of the century, the early feminist movement concentrated on winning the right for women to vote in government elections, and the right to own property. Women in New Zealand were first given the vote at the end of the 19th century, but other countries were slow to follow. Some women used peaceful ways to attract attention, while others used more physical tactics, such as chaining themselves to railings, or attacking the police or politicians.

By the end of the 1920s, women in Norway, the USA, Denmark, Britain, Germany and the USSR could vote in elections. But France and Italy did not change their voting laws until 1945 and 1946, and in Switzerland, women did not have a vote until 1971. Even today there are still parts of the world, such

*French feminist Simone de Beauvoir*

as Saudi Arabia and Kuwait, where only men can vote.

The next objective was to fight for social and economic rights, such as equal pay and equal job opportunities. The Women's Liberation Movement of the 1960s sought a complete transformation of society, which they claimed had been shaped by men throughout history. In many countries, it was made illegal to discriminate against women in housing, education or employment.

*Indira Gandhi, prime minister of India*

## HUMAN RIGHTS

In 1948, the General Assembly of the UN drew up a list of rights that governments should grant to their citizens. It was called the Universal Declaration of Human Rights. The various points included freedom of speech and religion, and the right to education and work.

When the Declaration failed to ensure all its points, a number of pressure groups were established. The largest, Amnesty International, was founded in 1961, to help those whose rights were being ignored.

*Poster calling for support for Amnesty*

*Amnesty symbol*

By 1980, it had over 200,000 members in 40 countries. Other groups dedicated to the cause of human rights include the International Committee of the Red Cross and the International Committee of Jurists. These groups engage in research, publish reports and put pressure on governments that do not respect human rights.

Human rights have been central to the demands for democracy of opposition groups in Latin America, China and

*Women waiting to present a human rights petition in El Salvador*

South Africa. In the USA, black civil rights groups fought for, and won, more rights for the African-American population. In the 1970s, human rights groups emerged in the Eastern bloc. They aimed to publicize the failure of communist governments to ensure basic rights for their people. They played an important role in the breakdown of communism in 1989 and 1990 (see pages 68-71).

## THE GREEN MOVEMENT

In the 1960s, a number of organizations, known as green groups, formed to publicize the harm being done to the Earth and the need to reduce the waste created by modern society (see pages 76-7). Some members wanted to reject industrial society altogether and to return to a peasant-like existence.

In the 1970s and 1980s, as scientists revealed more about the extent of the damage, these groups gained enough support to form their own political parties. At the same time, "green" parties began to influence ruling political parties in western countries. Governments began to take environmental matters more seriously. This has led to negotiations and treaties on green issues.

*A blue whale, one of the world's endangered species*

*In 1985, the French government sank the Greenpeace boat "Rainbow Warrior" for trying to stop nuclear testing.*

# The environment

In the 20th century, a great deal of damage has been done to the planet. In the 1970s and 1980s, pressure groups, known as green groups, began to publicize their fears. Governments reacted to public concern by introducing policies to limit pollution and other forms of destruction.

## ACID RAIN, FUMES AND OIL SPILLAGE

One of the most damaging types of pollution is "acid rain". This is formed when chemicals from industries and vehicle exhausts are released into the air and mix with clouds to pollute rainfall. Acid rain strips trees bare and poisons plants and animals.

Industries and motor vehicles churn out smoke which pollutes the air. Some measures have been drawn up to prevent this, but smog (smoky fog found in cities) continues to get worse. Disasters like the chemical spillage in 1984 in India, when 2000 people were poisoned by gas, and the Chernobyl nuclear spill, add to the problem. Oil spillages also cause damage. In 1989, the US oil tanker *Exxon Valdez* ran aground, pouring millions of barrels of oil into the sea. In 1991, two million barrels of oil leaked into the Persian Gulf during the Gulf War.

Cars and factories burn coal and oil.

Gases and fumes mix with rain clouds.

Acid rain falls and strips the land of vegetation.

*This shows the way that acid rain forms.*

## THE OZONE LAYER

The ozone layer, which protects the Earth from the Sun's harmful ultraviolet rays, is steadily thinning. This is due to the use of what scientists call ozone-depleting substances, such as CFC gases found in aerosols, glues and refrigerators. In 1982, scientists first noticed that the ozone layer over Antarctica had become very thin. People are worried by this, because it leads to an increase in skin cancer.

The UN has agreed that the use of CFCs should be phased out. From 1986 to 1992, CFC use dropped by 40%. Unfortunately some of the substances used to replace CFCs are also ozone depleters.

*A CFC-packed aerosol can*

## GLOBAL WARMING

The world's average temperature is getting hotter, a trend known as "global warming". This is caused by the release of "greenhouse gases" into the air from burning fossil fuels, such as coal and oil. These gases trap warm air on the surface of the Earth, in the way that a greenhouse keeps in heat. The burning of rainforests, and the fumes from vehicles both increase the levels of carbon dioxide, the most dangerous greenhouse gas. The temperature rise may one day cause some areas to become deserts and others to be submerged under the sea, as rainfall levels drop and polar icebergs melt.

*This diagram shows how global warming builds up.*

Some of the Sun's heat is reflected safely back.

Burning fossil fuels and forests releases greenhouse gases.

The sun's heat is trapped close to the Earth by the greenhouse gases.

## THE RAINFORESTS

Large areas of forest are disappearing. Some are burned to create more land for agriculture. Others are felled to make paper, or for firewood. Tropical rainforests, which grow in warm rainy areas, have been especially badly hit. Rainforests help to control the Earth's climate and rainfall, because leaves trap rain, and then release water back into the air. When rainforests burn, they release carbon dioxide which is a greenhouse gas. In the 1980s, over 10% of the rainforests were destroyed.

Apart from the effects on climate and atmosphere, many plants and animals will die out if forests are destroyed. 25% of medicines use rainforest ingredients. It is likely that treatments for AIDS and cancer will use such ingredients.

Many tribes have lived in the forests for thousands of years, but now their livelihoods are threatened. One of the most affected groups is the Yanomami tribe in Brazil. Their land is being taken away by farmers and cattle ranchers, while the rivers they wash in and drink from are being polluted. In 1500, there were 5 million native people in Brazil, but today there are less than 200,000.

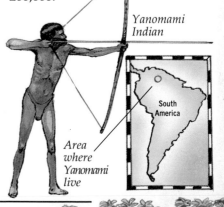

*Yanomami Indian*

*Area where Yanomami live*

South America

*This picture shows the ways in which rainforests contribute to the world.*

Carbon dioxide

Oxygen

Trees take in poisonous carbon dioxide and convert it into oxygen.

Rainforest leaves trap rain and release it back into the air. When trees are cut down, rainfall decreases.

A great hornbill

Rainforest plants, often used in medicines

Burning trees release carbon dioxide into the atmosphere.

The felling of trees leads to soil erosion.

## EXTINCTION

The destruction of natural habitats, combined with the world trade in animals, has led to a decline in wildlife. Certain species have become extinct, or face extinction.

*All these species are at risk from total extinction.*

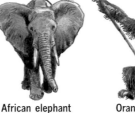
African elephant

Orang-utan

Rhino

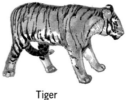
Tiger

Mountain gorilla

Jaguar

## SOLUTIONS

Although much damage has been done already, there are things that people can do to slow down the destruction, and even to create new life in areas where it has been destroyed in the past.

Only a quarter of the world's people live in rich countries, but each year they use three quarters of the world's energy resources, so creating the most pollution. Efforts to save energy, by using less electricity, using bicycles or public transport instead of cars and recycling waste products, help to slow down the damage.

Governments have begun to work together to reduce the harm being done to the environment. In 1992, the first UN "Earth Summit" was held in Rio de Janeiro, Brazil. Members of 150 governments signed two major agreements. The first dealt with the problem of climatic change and made new laws to prevent global warming. The other, known as the Bio-Diversity Convention, aimed to protect the world's plant and animal species. Members also agreed to set up a permanent UN body to make sure that these measures are applied. The summit helped raise awareness of issues and showed that governments could work together.

*The UN banned drift net fishing for tuna as it leads to the trapping and killing of dolphins.*

# Facing the future

As the year 2000 approaches, the advances and setbacks of the century can be reviewed, and predictions can be made about the likely changes to come. Works of science fiction have been written, predicting strange future worlds, ruled by robots, aliens, only men, only women, apes or computers. Writers and film directors imagine eternal life, computers with human intelligence, faster forms of travel, and even teleportation (disappearing from one place and reappearing in another).

Much prediction verges on fantasy, but experts agree that trends such as computerization, mechanization, population growth and medical improvements will continue. It is hoped that the 21st century will also bring more efficient use of renewable resources, less damage to the environment, and less hunger and poverty.

Many environmental, political and economic problems remain, but governments are starting to work together to solve them.

*The General Motors "Ultralite" made in 1991*

*Smaller frontal area to minimize wind drag*

*Wheels with low rolling resistance*

*Biosphere 2 in the Arizona desert, USA. It is a $160 million project to try to maintain life in a scientifically controlled and created atmosphere.*

## POPULATION

World population has doubled since 1956 and now stands at around five and a half billion. There are more people alive now than have ever died in the past. The population expands by over 97 million people a year, 85 million of whom are in poorer developing countries in the third world, while some of the countries in Europe are barely experiencing any growth at all. In some places, the population is actually getting smaller.

The greatest disadvantage of high population growth is that it leads to greater pressure on the economy and on the land's natural resources. Poor countries cannot support high levels of population, yet many people choose to have large families, because they want children to provide for them in their old age. Generally people are living longer, and fewer children are dying at birth, or in infancy. The national government of China, the country with the world's biggest population, has tried to solve the problem of growth by introducing measures to encourage families to have only one child. Despite this, the population still expands by millions each year.

Experts believe that if women in poorer countries had better access to education and birth control techniques, the birthrate would decline, much as it has done in the developed world.

*A Chinese poster encouraging parents to have only one child*

## THE THIRD WORLD

Originally, the idea of a "third world" began in the Cold War era. The term referred to all countries not allied to the USA and the West, called the first world, or the Soviet bloc, known as the second world. The term came to be used to describe countries in which the majority of the population earn little and have a low standard of living. In these countries, there tends to be much greater extremes of rich and poor. Many more people die of starvation, because not enough food is produced and distributed, or disease, because often the water is not clean.

*Children operating a water pump in Africa*

Lightweight frame and body

*Ethiopian refugees walking over the mountains in search of more fertile land*

Poverty is measured in different ways. The average annual income per person is one indication of the wealth of a nation. For example, in Mozambique this is $80, while in Switzerland it is $30,000. Studies also look at rates of infant mortality, life expectancy, food supplies and the number of people per doctor.

The term "Third World" is misleading, because it lumps various countries into one group. In fact, they are very different from each other. China, Brazil and Mexico are industrial and urban, while African nations tend to be more rural.

## DISASTERS

Natural disasters, such as earthquakes, hurricanes, floods and droughts, have always occurred, but in the 20th century there have been man-made disasters which have added to existing problems. War and political instability have made many people homeless and starving.

These people become refugees, moving from one area to another. The Soviet invasion of Afghanistan led to five million people seeking places to live in Pakistan and Iran. Two million Palestinians were made homeless by the creation of Israel, and in Iraq, Kurdish people have been persecuted and expelled from the land.

## INTERNATIONAL RELATIONS

Governments and organizations around the world recognize the need for international aid agencies to intervene to help people in the poorer nations. UNICEF (run by the United Nations) and the Red Cross group provide money, food and medical supplies in emergency situations. Television has been effective in showing the rest of the world the horror of famine and has led to the foundation of many new fund-raising organizations. In 1984 and 1985, pop stars joined together to raise money with the "Band Aid" record and the "Live Aid" concert for Ethiopians and other African famine victims.

International development assistance from these sources amounts to over $50 billion every year. The USA and Japan are the largest donors. The countries which receive the most aid are China, Bangladesh, Israel, Pakistan and Kenya.

*The concert stage at Live Aid*

*The UN logo*

*The UNICEF logo*

*The Red Cross logo*

In the 1970s, western banks lent large sums of money to countries in the developing world. By the 1980s, it became clear that many of these countries were not able to pay back these debts. Often these nations have have put all their resources into paying off their debts, and the interest charged on the loan has become bigger than the loan itself.

Foreign aid has not been able to solve long-term problems. Experts suggest that economic patterns need to be changed instead. In addition to these problems, political difficulties within and between countries continue. All over the world, countries are dividing up into smaller states. This creates tensions between religious and nationalist groups, which can result in war, as has happened in the ex-Yugoslavia. Both political and economic patterns will continue to change well into the 21st century.

# Glossary

**Abdication**
The giving up of a throne or power.

**Alliance**
Formal agreement, often military, between two or more countries.

**Annex**
To join one area to a larger territory by conquering or occupying it.

**Anti-Semitism**
Persecution, hatred and discrimination of Jews.

**Armistice**
Agreement between enemies in a war to cease fighting to discuss peace terms.

**Autocracy**
Government by a person or group, with unlimited authority, where no opposition is allowed.

**Bolshevik**
Originally a Russian communist supporter of Lenin, working with the aim of immediate revolution. Later used as a general term to describe a communist.

**Capitalism**
An economic system where the means of production (industries, factories and businesses) are owned by a relatively small group, who provide the investment and take a large share of the profits.

**Censorship**
Policy of restricting the freedom of speech or thought expressed in plays, books, etc. usually for political reasons.

**Christianity**
Religion based on the life and teachings of Jesus Christ.

**CIA**
The US Central Intelligence Agency, created in 1947 to coordinate and oversee American spying and secret political activities.

**Civil disobedience**
A non-violent way of protesting and trying to achieve political change by refusing to follow the laws of a country.

**Civil rights**
The equality in social, economic and political matters.

**Coalition**
A temporary alliance between diffferent groups or political parties, for instance in a government.

**Collectivization**
The organization of the ownership of the means of production by the state into groups, or collectives.

**Colonization**
A country or area of land held and ruled over by another country, sometimes by force.

**Commonwealth**
The organization made up of former member countries of the British empire, with the aim of mutual cooperation and assistance.

**Communism**
An ideology mainly based on the ideas of Karl Marx, which promotes a society without social classes, in which private ownership has been abolished. A system where the means of production are owned by the state.

**Conscription**
Compulsory military service, often introduced during wars.

**Constitution**
The fixed political principles on which a state is ruled and governed.

**Coup d'état**
The sudden overthrow of an existing government, usually by a small group, often made up of army officers.

**Decolonization**
The process by which a colony is made independent from its ruling country.

**Democracy**
An system of government originating in Ancient Greece, meaning "rule by the people".

**Democractic Party**
One of two major political parties in the USA. It tends to put a greater emphasis on the activities and powers of the central government.

**Depression**
A period when industrial and economic activity falls, usually associated with high unemployment, as in the Great Depression of the 1930s.

**Dictatorship**
Non-royal autocratic rule, in which the leader's position is imposed by force.

**Disarmament**
Arms and weapon reduction, which can be unilateral (carried out by one country) or multilateral (based on agreed reductions between countries).

**Dissident**
A person who publicly disagrees with the government and is often exiled or persecuted for this disagreement.

**Dominion status**
Term describing the self-governing lands under the British empire.

**Dynasty**
A sequence of hereditary rulers.

**Economy**
The term used to describe the system of distribution, buying and selling of goods and services in a country.

**Emigration**
Leaving one place to settle in another.

**Ethnic groups**
People linked together by their race, religion, language or other features.

**Extremism**
The belief and promotion of extreme political ideas.

**Fascism**
An ideology first developed by Mussolini. A form of government which allows no rival political parties and which controls the lives of its citizens. Nazism is a form of fascism.

**Federation**
A type of government in which power is shared between a central parliament and several regional governments.

**Fundamentalism**
Strict, inflexible religious beliefs.

**Glasnost**
Policy of openness and freedom developed in the USSR under the leadership of Gorbachev.

**Guerilla**
A fighter operating in secret, usually against the ruling government. From the Spanish *guerra*, meaning "war".

**Hinduism**
System of beliefs which make up the dominant religion of India. Hindus believe in many gods and reincarnation.

**Ideology**
A theory which sets out how a state should be run and what its political priorities should be.

**Independence**
When referring to a country or state, independence means the freedom from other countries in government and rule.

**Industrialization**
The development of a country's industries and factories, so that its economy is no longer based on farming.

**Inflation**
A large rise in the price of most goods and commodities.

**Islam**
Religion of Muslims, which is based on the life and teachings of the prophet Mohammed.

**Judaism**
The religion of the Jews founded on the history of the ancient area of Israel as recorded in the Bible.

**KGB**
The Committee for State Security in the USSR from 1954 until the break up of the Soviet Union. The KGB was responsible for security troops, secret services and spying.

**Left-wing**
A phrase which is used to describe any ideology that tends toward socialism or communism.

**Liberalism**
A set of beliefs which encourages individual freedom and maintains that governments should interfere as little as possible with people's lives.

**Martial law**
The rule of law established by military courts and maintained by soldiers, in the absence of non-military authority.

**Marxism**
Political theories following the teachings of the 19th century writer, Karl Marx. The belief that actions and institutions are determined by economics, that the class struggle is the instrument of change and that capitalism will be overcome by Communism.

**Minority rule**
Government by a group of people who are different, politically or racially, from the majority of the population.

**Monarchy**
Form of government in which authority is given to one person, a king or queen, who inherits the position.

**Nationalism**
Loyalty to one's own country, similar to patriotism, but which can sometimes be taken to extreme levels, often leading to national aggression against other counties.

**Neutrality**
A state of non-alliance to any side, especially during a war.

**Parliament**
An official meeting place for decision-making and law-giving.

**Perestroika**
Policy of restructuring and economic change in the USSR under Gorbachev.

**Propaganda**
Information broadcast to publicize aims and achievements of a particular political group.

**Protectorate**
A territory largely controlled by, but not annexed to, a more powerful nation.

**Psychology**
Scientific study of the way that animals and humans behave.

**Puppet state**
A country that appears to be independent but in reality is being ruled by another country.

**Racism**
The belief that a race of people has separate and unique characteristics that make it superior to other races, and so can often lead to aggression and hatred between races.

**Radical**
Tending to extreme or fundamental social, political or economic changes or beliefs.

**Referendum**
A general vote among people on a single issue of importance.

**Refugees**
People fleeing from persecution or war.

**Republic**
A state governed by the representatives of the people, without a king, queen or any sort of autocratic ruler.

**Republican Party**
One of two major political parties in the USA, which usually emphasizes the rights of the individual over those of the state.

**Right-wing**
Conservative ideology in which change is opposed and the traditional way of doing things is encouraged.

**Sanctions**
When one country stops part or all of its economic, trade or cultural links with another country as a way of putting pressure on it.

**Segregation**
The policy of creating very separate facilities and rules for one ethnic or minority group.

**Self-government**
The government of a country by its own people.

**Socialism**
An ideology that stresses equality of income and wealth, and believes in public (state) ownership of industries (the means of production).

**Soviet**
An elected government council or trade union in the USSR. Generally the word is used as an adjective meaning "of the USSR".

**Stalinism**
Policies and methods associated with the rule of Josef Stalin, often involving terrorism and repression.

**Terrorism**
The use of terror, for instance bombing attacks and assassinations, as a means of political persuasion.

**Trade unions**
Collections of workers who combine to state their grievances to employers, and to improve working conditions.

**Zionism**
Political movement which campaigned for the establishment of a Jewish homeland in Palestine. After the foundation of Israel, Zionists became concerned with maintaining the state and encouraging growth.

# Who's who of 20th century people

## Ali, Mohammad (1942- )
Heavyweight boxing champion. Born Cassius Clay, Ali is considered to be the finest heavyweight boxer of all time. He held the world title from 1964 to 1967, from 1974-78, and in 1979. He is remembered for his flamboyance in the ring and his black Muslim politics, which led to his title being taken away in 1967.

## Amundsen, Roald (1872-1928)
Norwegian explorer. In 1911, Amundsen led the first successful expedition to the South Pole, in Antarctica, narrowly beating a British party. He was also the first person to navigate the Northwest Passage in the South Arctic Ocean.

## Arafat, Yasser (1929- )
Leader of the Palestine Liberation Organization. In 1968, Arafat became leader of the Palestine Liberation Organization, which uses political and guerilla tactics to campaign for the creation of a separate Palestinian state. In 1993, he began peace negotiations with Israeli leaders.

## Astaire, Fred (1899-1987)
US dancer and film star. In the 1930s, Astaire made a series of musicals, such as *Top Hat* (1935), which featured him tap-dancing with his partner Ginger Rogers. That partnership came to an end in 1935, but he continued to be one of the world's most popular stars in films such as *Easter Parade* (1948) and *Silk Stockings* (1957).

## Atatürk, Kemal (1881-1938)
Turkish president and reformer. The name Atatürk means "father of the Turks". He led an army against the occupying Greeks after the First World War, and in 1923 became the first president of the new republic of Turkey. Once in power, he introduced radical reforms to make Turkey more like other European countries. The old Arabic alphabet, for instance, was replaced by the Latin one.

## Bandaranaike, Sirimavo (1916- )
Sri Lankan prime minister. In 1960, Bandaranaike succeeded her husband to become the world's first woman prime minister. She held this position in Sri Lanka for 12 years in the 1960s and 1970s, following nationalist and socialist policies.

## The Beatles
Successful and influential British pop group. The Beatles were four musicians, born in the 1940s, who became popular in the 1960s with hit songs, such as *Yesterday* and *Hey Jude,* and the album *Sergeant Pepper's Lonely Hearts Club Band*. They split up in 1969, and in 1980, John Lennon, who had written many of their finest songs, was shot and killed in New York.

## Samuel Beckett (1906-1989)
Irish playwright. Beckett wrote many novels, but it was his 1952 play, *Waiting for Godot,* that established him as an important force in 20th century thought and literature. It is about two tramps who wait in vain for a mysterious character called Godot, and was a comment on what Beckett saw as the hopelessness and emptiness of life. This and his subsequent plays have been translated and performed in many different languages around the world.

## Begin, Menachem (1913- )
Israeli prime minister. Originally from Russian Poland, Begin was leader of an Israeli terrorist group. He became prime minister in 1977. The following year, he negotiated a treaty with Anwar Sadat of Egypt to work for peace between Muslims and Jews. He shared the Nobel prize for peace with Sadat.

## Benes, Edvard (1884-1948)
Co-founder of Czechoslovakia in 1919. Benes served in most of the interwar governments before becoming president in 1935. The Nazis forced him to resign in 1938, while the communists did the same in 1948.

## Ben-Gurion, David (1886-1973)
Israel's first prime minister. Ben-Gurion became leader when the state of Israel was first formed in 1948, and held on to this position for 13 years. His policies remained influential after his death.

## Bergman, Ingmar (1918- )
Swedish film director. Since 1949, Bergman has made 43 films, such as *The Seventh Seal* (1956), *Wild Strawberries* (1957), and *Fanny and Alexander* (1983), which have won him awards and international fame. The issues that he deals with - death, God, life and love - have influenced many other film directors and writers.

## Biko, Stephen (1946-77)
South African civil rights leader. In 1968, Biko became the president of the South African Students Organization, and was active in campaigning against the white rulers and apartheid. In 1977, he was arrested and brutally killed in police custody. His early death has made him a hero and a symbol of the black struggle for equal rights.

## Brandt, Willy (1913-1992)
West German statesman. Chancellor of the Federal Republic of Germany from 1969 to 1974, Brandt's renown lies in his attempts to improve relations with the Eastern bloc. In 1980, he chaired the Brandt Commission on the world economy, and was critical of the role of rich countries in the third world.

## Brezhnev, Leonid (1906-1982)
Soviet leader from 1968 to 1982. Brezhnev followed an aggressive foreign policy, but inside the USSR there was economic stagnation.

## Brown, James (1928- )
US soul singer. His song *Please, please, please* is considered to be the first soul record and established Brown as an important musician. Most dance songs use elements of his music, and his dancing has been widely copied. In 1988, he was arrested for assault and possessing a gun. He was sentenced to prison for six years, but was released in 1991.

## Callas, Maria (1923-1977)
Greek opera singer. Callas combined a dramatic soprano voice and fine acting abilities, to make her one of the world's greatest opera singers. She concentrated on early Italian opera and Verdi.

## Capone, Al (1899-1947)
1920s US gangster. From 1919, Capone built up a huge criminal empire in Chicago. When the US government banned alcohol, Capone started selling it illegally. In 1929, his gang killed five rivals in the notorious St. Valentine's Day Massacre. His crimes were never proven, so it was not until 1931 that he was imprisoned on the lesser charge of non-payment of taxes.

## Caruso, Enrico (1873-1921)
Italian opera singer. Caruso was one of the first major tenors to be recorded on gramophone and packed concert halls across Europe and the USA.

### Castro, Fidel (1927- )

Communist president of Cuba. In 1959, after two previous attempts, Castro led a successful revolution against General Batista, the dictator of Cuba. Castro became leader of a socialist government and defended Cuba against a US-supported attack by Cuban exiles at the Bay of Pigs in 1961. He has been leader ever since, passing measures in 1976 to increase his power.

### Ceausescu, Nicolae (1918-1989)

Romanian dictator for 20 years. Ceausescu rose to the leadership of the Communist party in 1969. He made the country more independent from the USSR and the rest of the Eastern bloc. It was not until 1989, that his regime was fully revealed to the world. Ceausescu lived in great luxury in a palace he had made, while many Romanians starved. Following a popular revolt, Ceausescu and his wife, Elena, were executed by firing squad on Christmas day, 1989.

### Chanel, Coco (1883-1971)

French fashion designer. In the 1920s, Chanel revolutionized women's clothes by introducing softer, more comfortable shapes and fabrics. She designed sweaters, which had previously only been worn by workers and made suntans fashionable. In the 1950s, she introduced the classic fitted Chanel suit, which became a uniform for rich, stylish women. Her perfumes, such as Chanel no.5, continue to sell across the world.

### Chaplin, Charlie (1889-1977)

Film star. Chaplin was born in London, but made his name in Hollywood. He appeared in his first silent film in 1914. Two of his most successful films, *The Kid* (1920) and *The Gold Rush* (1925), starred Chaplin as the "little tramp" character, complete with bowler hat, cane and moustache. He refused to make talking pictures and, in the 1930s, it became difficult for his silent films to compete at the box office. In 1952, he was exiled from the USA, charged with having communist ideas.

### Churchill, Winston (1874-1965)

British prime minister. A leading British politician for over 60 years, Churchill is best known for his premiership during the Second World War. He always recognized the danger Hitler posed and thought that only war would stop him. He played a major role in the peace conferences after the war.

### Dalai Lama (1935- )

Tibetan religious leader. Believed by his people to be the reincarnation of a Buddhist god, the Dalai Lama ruled Tibet until occupation by China in 1950. Since then he has lived in exile and acted as his country's spokesperson in the fight for independence.

### Dali, Salvador (1904-1989)

Spanish surrealist painter. Dali had a talent for painting, self-publicity and growing elaborate moustaches. From the 1930s, he became influenced by the writings of Sigmund Freud and began to paint dream-like scenes in a very realistic style. From the 1950s, many of his paintings had religious themes.

### de Beauvoir, Simone (1908-1986)

French writer and feminist. Although, she was a well-known novelist and intellectual, de Beauvoir's fame rests largely on *The Second Sex* (1949), which was an important feminist work. In it, she argued that motherhood and marriage imprisoned women.

### de Gaulle, Charles (1890-1970)

French president. When France was invaded by German troops in 1940, de Gaulle escaped to England to lead the French resistance movement. After the liberation of France, he became President for a short time, but in 1953 retired from politics. He was asked to become president in 1958 and was given very wide powers. He helped to achieve France's economic recovery and held onto power when under attack during the workers' and students' unrest in May 1968.

### de Valera, Eamon (1882-1975)

Irish statesman, prime minister and president. Until the 1920s, Ireland was still part of the British Isles. De Valera fought for independence and was imprisoned by the British. When Irish independence was granted, de Valera became prime minister, and then president of the Republic in 1959.

### Diaghilev, Sergei (1871-1929)

Ballet innovator. In 1909, he formed his first ballet company, which starred two of the greatest dancers ever, Anna Pavlova and Vaslav Nijinsky. This new company broke away from old conventions . The steps were new and different, the sets designed by abstract artists, and the music was by experimental new composers such as Stravinsky. Diaghilev changed the way ballet was produced.

### DiMaggio, Joe (1914- )

US baseball player. Known to many only for his brief marriage to Marilyn Monroe, DiMaggio was in fact so good a player that he defied probability and history. In 1941, he made at least one hit in 56 successive games. This is the greatest record ever and has never been matched.

### Disney, Walt (1901-66)

US cartoonist and film producer. In 1923, Disney made his first animated film, but it was not until 1927, with the introduction of Mickey Mouse, that his cartoons became successful. Mickey was joined by others such as Pluto, Goofy and Donald Duck. Disney's company also made cartoon of classic fairy tales, such as *Snow White and the Seven Dwarfs* (1938) and *Beauty and the Beast* (1992). His empire is further known for its theme parks, Disneyland, Disneyworld and Eurodisney.

### Einstein, Albert (1879-1955)

German-born Jewish physicist. In 1905, Einstein published four papers, including his Special Theory of Relativity, which revolutionized 20th century physics. He continued to work in Germany on his theories until 1933, when Hitler came to power. Einstein escaped to the USA. After 1945, he campaigned against the use of the atomic bomb that his theories and discoveries had made possible.

### Eisenstein, Sergei (1898-1948)

Russian film director. With his three 1920s films celebrating the 1917 Russian revolution, *Strike, Battleship Potemkin* and *October*, Eisenstein developed his influential film techniques. *Battleship Potemkin* is generally acknowledged by critics to be the finest film ever made.

### Eliot, T. S. (1888-1965)

Poet, critic and playwright. In 1915, Eliot published his first poem *The Love Song of J. Alfred Prufrock*. This became a popular work, but it was *The Wasteland* (1922) that established him as an important modern poet. His plays have also been much performed.

### Franco, Francisco (1892-1975)

Spanish dictator. After the fascist victory in the Spanish Civil War (1936-1939), Franco became the leader of the government. He made himself head of state for life and nominated Prince Juan Carlos as his successor. His regime became more liberal near the end.

### Freud, Sigmund (1856-1939)

Austrian Jewish psychiatrist. In the 1890s, Freud used new techniques of analysis to get patients to reveal thoughts that the mind might be supressing. In 1899, he published *The Intepretation of Dreams*, which analyzed dreams in terms of experiences and desires dating from childhood. When Austria was annexed by Germany, Freud left for London to avoid persecution.

### Gandhi, Indira (1917-1984)

Prime minister of India. The daughter of the first prime minister of India, Indira Gandhi became prime minister herself for much of the 1960s and 1970s. She failed to end religious unrest and was assassinated by a Sikh bodyguard in 1984. She was succeeded by her son, Rajiv, who was assassinated in 1991.

### Gandhi, Mohandas K. (1869-1948)

Indian nationalist leader. Gandhi played a huge role in winning India's independence from Britain. He followed a policy of civil disobedience (non-violent resistance) to achieve change. He agreed to the partition of the sub-continent into India and Pakistan, although he had always hoped that they would remain united.

### Garbo, Greta (1905-1990)

Film star. Garbo was born in Sweden and came to Hollywood in 1925. She made a series of silent films, where her beauty and allure made her very popular. She successfully made the transition to talking films, but retired in 1941 when one of her films was badly received. She became a recluse and was hardly ever seen, making her an even more legendary figure.

### Garcia Marquez, Gabriel (1928- )

Colombian novelist. The publication of *One Hundred Years of Solitude*, in 1967, introduced Garcia Marquez's style of writing to the world. Often called "magic realism", he mixes reality, folk stories and fantasy. He won a Nobel prize for literature in 1982 and published *Love in the Time of Cholera* in 1986.

### Gershwin, George (1898-1937)

US composer and pianist. In 1919, Gershwin made his name with the jazz song *Swanee,* and in 1924 wrote the successful musical *Lady Be Good*. In the same year, he expanded into the world of orchestral music by mixing jazz and romantic piano in *Rhapsody in Blue*. He later experimented further with *Porgy and Bess,* a African-American folk opera.

### Gorbachev, Mikhail (1931- )

Reforming Soviet president. Having been active in communist party politics since 1970, Gorbachev became general secretary of the Party and leader of the USSR in 1985. He introduced wide-ranging policies, radically reforming the economy and government. In 1991, he was deposed by hardline communists, briefly regained power and then became jobless when the USSR broke up into separate states.

### Graham, Billy (1918- )

US Christian evangelical preacher. By the 1950s, Graham was holding huge mass rallies on every continent. His message of a return to Christian values, old-fashioned morality and the power of faith to heal has been very popular with those who feel disturbed by modern life. In the 1990s, he continues to attract huge audiences.

### Greer, Germaine (1939- )

Australian feminist writer. The publication of *The Female Eunuch* in the 1970s established Greer as a leading figure in the Women's Liberation Movement. She argued that women were frustrated by male-dominated society.

### Guevara, Che (1928-1967)

Argentinian revolutionary. Best remembered for his part in the Cuban revolution, Guevara believed that violent action should be used to liberate third world countries. He was involved in guerilla action in Cuba, the Congo and Bolivia, and was executed by Bolivian soldiers.

### Haile Selassie I (1892-1975)

Emperor of Ethiopia. From 1930 until the Italian invasion in 1935, Haile Selassie ruled over one of the only African countries that was free from European domination. After his restoration to power in 1941, he set out to modernize the country, and was central to the movement for African unity. He was overthrown in a coup in 1975. He is thought of as divine by people who follow the Rastafarian religion.

### Havel, Vaclav (1936- )

Czech playwright and president. Before becoming a politician, Havel was known as a radical playwright who questioned the communist government in Czechoslovakia. He was imprisoned for his part in forming the human rights group Charter 77. He emerged as the people's leader during the "velvet revolution" of 1989 and became the president. Havel presided over the division of the area into two countries, the Czech lands and Slovakia, in 1992.

### Hawking, Stephen (1942- )

British physicist. Despite having a wasting disease that confines him to a wheelchair and makes unaided speech impossible, Hawking is one of the world's most important modern scientists. *A Brief History of Time,* which deals with Big Bang Theory, was a surprise bestseller, and he proved that black holes do radiate energy.

### Heyerdahl, Thor (1914- )

Norwegian historian and voyager. Heyerdahl wanted to prove that South Americans sailed to Polynesia in 500AD. To do this he built a wooden raft, as they would have had, and made the journey in 101 days. The hazardous trip was recounted in the best selling book *The Kon-Tiki Expedition* (1948). He continued to make similar crossings to prove historical theories.

### Hirohito (1901-1989)

Japanese emperor. Before 1946, Japanese emperors were thought to have divine powers and knowledge which could not be questioned. After the Second World War, Hirohito, emperor since 1926, gave up these powers and helped modernize Japan.

### Hitler, Adolf (1889-1945)

German dictator. Born in Austria, Hitler rose to power in Germany, by promising to restore the country to glory. From 1933 to 1939, he ruthlessly suppressed all opposition at home. His invasions of Austria, Czechoslovakia and Poland led to the Second World War. When the Allies won in 1945, Hitler committed suicide. During the war, Hitler put into practice his extreme ideas about racial superiority. Millions of Jews, gypsies, homosexuals and other groups hated by Hitler and the Nazis were imprisoned and murdered.

### Ho Chi Minh (1890-1969)

Vietnamese leader. After the Second World War. Ho Chi Minh led the communist Vietnam League for Independence against French colonial rule. In 1954, his forces beat the French army and he declared himself president of the republic in the north. He led communist forces against the USA and the south Vietnamese in the Vietnam War. The old capital city of Saigon is now named after him.

## Jackson, Michael (1958- )

US pop star. In the late 1960s, the young Michael Jackson achieved fame as the lead singer of a family group called the Jackson Five. He went on to have a very successful solo career, with his dance albums *Off the Wall* (1979), *Thriller* (1982) and *Bad* (1987). *Thriller* was the most successful album of all time. His on-stage brilliance is sometimes overshadowed by his off-stage eccentricity, but he continues to pack stadiums all over the world.

## Jiang Jie Shi (1887-1975)

Chinese revolutionary leader. In 1911, Jiang took part in political activities against the ancient ruling Manchu dynasty of China. After years of civil unrest, Jiang became president of China in 1928. He maintained his leadership during the Japanese invasion (1938-1945) but afterwards lost control to the communists. He then moved his government to the small island of Taiwan, where he encouraged industrial and economic growth.

## Jinnah, Mohammed (1876-1948)

First governor-general of Pakistan. A member of the Indian National Congress since 1906, Jinnah campaigned for a separate Muslim state in the Indian subcontinent. When Pakistan (the area mainly populated by Muslims) was created in 1947, Jinnah became its first governor-general and died in office.

## Kafka, Franz (1883-1924)

Czech writer and novelist. In a life cut short by tuberculosis, Kafka produced many short stories. They were published after his death, despite the fact that he had asked for them to be burned. The guilty, nightmarish quality to stories such as *The Trial* and *Metamorphosis* (about a man who wakes to find he has been inexplicably turned into a beetle) established Kafka as one of the great writers of the 20th century.

## Kennedy, John F. (1917-1963)

US president. Born into a wealthy Irish-American family, Kennedy became the first Roman Catholic to be elected president of the USA. He supported black civil rights groups and the poor, but also concentrated money and effort into costly anti-communist campaigns in Cuba and Indochina. He has become a legend for his reforms and because he was assassinated after only a thousand days of presidency.

## Kenyatta, Jomo (1889-1978)

Kenya's first president. Having spent many years in London, he returned to Kenya in 1946 and was made the leader of the Kenya African Union, fighting for independence from Britain. He was imprisoned for nine years by the British government, who accused him of involvement in the Mau Mau risings of 1952. He became president of the republic of Kenya in 1964.

## Keynes, John Maynard (1883-1946)

Influential British economist. During the First World War, Keynes was a government advisor, and later worked on peacetime policy. After the Second World War, he suggested the establishment of a world bank for clearing international debts, but his innovative plan was rejected. He overturned much of the established thinking on the problem of unemployment. Many economists believed that the economy would regulate itself, so that unemployment would only be temporary. Keynes argued that the government should stimulate demand by commissioning public works to create employment.

## Khomeini, Ayatollah (1900-1989)

Iranian religious and political leader. Khomeini was banished from Iran in 1964 for his extreme Islamic beliefs. In 1979, he returned to establish a new Islamic republic, replacing the old Shah of Iran. Under his regime, tension increased between Iran and nearby Iraq, and between Iran and the West.

## Khrushchev, Nikita (1894-1971)

Soviet leader from 1953 to 1964. Khrushchev criticized Stalin for the terror of his regime. Despite almost going to war with the USA in 1962, he promoted peace between the superpowers. He quarrelled with Chairman Mao of China and lost his leadership soon after.

## King, Billie Jean (1943- )

US tennis player. In all, King won eleven major singles titles. Her talent and skill helped to improve the standing of women's tennis. In 1973, she was challenged to a game by Bobby Riggs, who claimed that even the top women's player could not beat him. She easily won the match, and scored a point for women's sport.

## King, Martin Luther (1929-1968)

US civil rights campaigner. A Christian church minister, King was influenced by Gandhi's ideas of non-violent resistance. In the 1960s, he led many protests against segregation. Later he broadened his campaigns to include protests against war and poverty. He was assassinated in 1968.

## le Corbusier (1887-1965)

Swiss-born French architect. Le Corbusier wanted to use modern materials to produce high quality mass housing. In 1923, he designed a very plain house with concrete pillars which he described as "a machine for living in". After the Second World War, he produced an even more influential building, the *Unité d'Habitation*, in Marseilles, France, which was a block of flats for 1600 people. This building inspired many tower block copies.

## Malcolm X (1925-1965)

US Black Muslim civil rights leader. Unlike Martin Luther King, Malcolm X preached that blacks should arm themselves and use violence in the struggle for justice. He was eventually shot and killed by fellow black Muslims.

## Mandela, Nelson (1918- )

South African ANC leader. Mandela was imprisoned for life in 1964 for his campaigns against apartheid. He was released in 1990 and resumed his leadership, taking part in negotiations to end white minority rule in South Africa.

## Mao Zedong (1893-1976)

Chinese leader. In 1921, Mao helped to found the Chinese Communist Party. In 1949, the communists defeated the nationalists and Mao became chairman of the People's Republic of China. He launched policies to increase agricultural and industrial production in China. Instead, harvests were destroyed, which led to famine. In the mid-1960s, he launched the "Cultural Revolution", in which communist fanaticism was encouraged and thousands of people were killed as "enemies of the revolution". He built up a "cult of personality" that lasted until his death.

## Matisse, Henri (1969-1954)

French artist. In the 1900s, Matisse was part of the Fauves group who wanted to express themselves through bold shades and brushstrokes. Later his work became increasingly simple in form, including abstract pieces such as *The Snail* (1953) made from cut-out bits of paper.

### McCarthy, Joseph (1908-1957)

US anti-communist politician. His election to the Senate in 1946 gave McCarthy an audience for his violently anti-communist beliefs. His campaign became known as "McCarthyism" and involved accusing prominent people of having of communist sympathies. These accusations were often followed by trials, dubbed "witch-hunts", and some people were exiled from the USA. In 1954, television hearings exposed the weakness of his claims and McCarthyism was over.

### Monroe, Marilyn (1926-1962)

US film star. Born Norma Jean Baker, Monroe had a very unhappy childhood. After a modelling career, she became a film star, playing a number of dizzy, breathy-voiced women, in films such as *Gentlemen Prefer Blondes* (1953) and *Some Like it Hot* (1959). Her mysterious death, usually thought to be suicide, has made her an enduring symbol of the pressures of fame and beauty.

### Mussolini, Benito (1883-1945)

Italian dictator. In 1919, Mussolini founded the Italian Fascist Party, which came to power in 1922. He established total control over the economy, the police and the army. In the 1930s, he became a more aggressive leader, invading Ethiopia and allying himself with Adolf Hitler. He entered the Second World War with Germany, but in 1943, after many military losses, he was forced to resign. He was shot and hung in 1945 by Italian peasants.

### Nehru, Jawaharlal (1889-1964)

Prime minister of India. Nehru worked with Gandhi in the independence movement, the Indian National Congress. When India was given independence in 1947, Nehru was elected as its first prime minister. While in office, he encouraged India to maintain and pursue further and complete separation from the British empire. He remained in office until his death.

### Nixon, Richard (1913- )

Disgraced US president. While in office from 1969 to 1974, Nixon improved relations between the USA and the Communist bloc, so reducing the risk of war. He also withdrew US troops from the Vietnam War. These achievements were overshadowed by the Watergate Scandal, in which it was revealed that he had used illegal activities to ensure re-election. When this was discovered, he was forced to resign.

### Nkrumah, Kwame (1909-1972)

President of Ghana. In 1957, Nkrumah became the first black African to rule his country since the 19th century. He declared himself president for life in 1964, and banned all opposition. While visiting China in 1966, rivals took over government and Nkrumah was not allowed to return to Ghana.

### Nureyev, Rudolph (1939-92)

Soviet born ballet dancer and choreographer. Already famous with the Kirov Ballet company, Nureyev defected to Western Europe in 1961, to escape communism. He became a permanent guest at the Royal Ballet in London, where he began a famous partnership with Margot Fonteyn. He died of an AIDS related illness in 1992.

### Nyerere, Julius (1922- )

Tanzanian president. After campaigning for Tanzania's independence, Nyerere became president in 1964, a position he has held ever since. He has written many books about African socialism and its effect on economic development.

### Pelé (1940- )

Brazilian soccer star. Only 15 years old at the beginning of his professional career, Pelé went on to score 97 goals for Brazil in international matches. He appeared in four World Cup finals, and was a hero all around the world for his amazing skill and sportsmanship.

### Picasso, Pablo (1881-1973)

Spanish artist. Picasso revolutionized art more than once in the 20th century. In 1907, he and Georges Braque founded the Cubist movement, which sought new ways of representing shapes on canvas. In 1937, he painted one of his most important pictures, *Guernica*, as a reaction to the bombing of a small town during the Spanish Civil War. His ideas and paintings dominate modern art styles.

### Pol Pot (1928- )

Cambodian dictator. In 1975, Pol Pot led a group of communist guerillas called the Khmer Rouge, and seized power in Cambodia (now called Kampuchea). Pol Pot then began a huge plan to force city workers back into the country to work in the fields. To try to reverse modernization, he murdered many scientists and intellectuals. In all, it is estimated that up to a quarter of the population was massacred. He was overthrown when the country was invaded by the Vietnamese in 1979.

### Presley, Elvis (1935-1977)

US rock and roll singer. From 1954, Presley was a successful recording artist, releasing hits such as *Heartbreak Hotel, Blue Suede Shoes* and *Jailhouse Rock*. He combined white country music and black blues music to be a pioneer of rock and roll. In the 1960s, he appeared in 30 musical films, and in the 1970s gave many live performances at Las Vegas. He died of an accidental drug overdose in 1977.

### Quant, Mary (1934- )

British fashion designer. Mary Quant is often credited with having dressed the 1960s, as it was she who introduced the mini-skirt in 1966, which took skirt lengths to new heights. She also designed accessories and make-up.

### Reagan, Ronald (1911- )

US politician. Former actor and film star, Reagan became president in 1981. He reduced public spending, while promoting a tough stance against the USSR. These policies proved popular and he was re-elected with more votes than any president in US history. In his second term, however, economic conditions worsened. As a result, he and the Soviet leader, Gorbachev, agreed to reduce military capacities.

### Roosevelt, Franklin D. (1882-1945)

US president. Despite being crippled by polio, Roosevelt became US president in 1933. He promised to get the USA out of economic depression with what he dubbed "New Deal" policies. He commissioned public works to create employment. He steered his country through the Second World War.

### Rushdie, Salman (1947- )

British novelist of Indian origin. *Midnight's Children*, Rushdie's 1981 novel, was a success, but he is best known for his 1988 work, *The Satanic Verses*. Many Muslims found its presentation of the *Koran* (the Islamic holy book) offensive. They burned his book and threatened him. He was condemned to death by the Ayatollah Khomeini, and he has been in hiding ever since.

### Sadat, Anwar (1918-1981)

President of Egypt (1970-81). Sadat made great progress in trying to end tensions in the Middle East. He entered into peace negotiations with Begin of Israel and they shared a Nobel peace prize. He was killed by Muslim extremists in 1981.

**Saddam Hussein (1937- )**
President of Iraq since 1979. Saddam Hussein involved his country in two major wars. The first, against Iraq, lasted eight years and exhausted both countries. The second, which began in 1990 when Iraqi forces invaded Kuwait, involved armies from outside the Middle East, including France, the USA and Britain. Inside Iraq, he uses violence and oppression against opposition groups.

**Stalin, Josef (1879-1953)**
Soviet dictator. Having played a small part in the 1917 Russian Revolution and Civil War, Stalin became general-secretary of the Communist Party in 1922, a position he held until his death. He introduced policies to bring all industry and agriculture under the control of the government. Stalin was ruthless in getting rid of opposition, by executions, massacres and purges. In 1945, he secured the direct or indirect control of territory in eastern Europe, and continued to govern this huge area until his death.

**Stopes, Marie (1880-1958)**
British birth control pioneer. In 1918, Marie Stopes produced two books which dealt with sex and contraception, both of which shocked the Catholic Church and the medical profession. In 1921, she established a birth control clinic in London, and within 30 years her work had been widely copied and accepted. She is thought to have done more than anyone else to control the potential population explosion in 20th century Europe.

**Stravinsky, Igor (1882-1971)**
Russian composer. After studying music in St.Petersburg, Stravinsky began composing works for Diaghilev's ballet company. In 1913, his ballet *The Rite of Spring* was first performed. Its rhythms and subject matter were so new and different that there was a riot at the theatre. He continued to compose and experiment with music in Switzerland, France and the USA.

**Mother Teresa (1910- )**
Albanian nun and charity worker. In 1948, Mother Teresa founded the Order of Missionaries of Charity to go among the poor of India, giving food and medicine to orphaned children. At first her work was in Calcutta alone, but her order has now established 700 shelters and clinics around the world. In 1979, she won the Nobel Peace prize.

**Thatcher, Margaret (1925- )**
British prime minister. Having been a member of the British parliament for 20 years, Thatcher became prime minister in 1979. She was known as the "Iron Lady" for her tough right-wing politics. Public spending was cut to lower the rate of inflation. Despite high unemployment, she was re-elected twice and became the longest serving prime minister for two centuries.

**Tito, Josip (1892-1980)**
Yugoslav president. When Yugoslavia was invaded by Germany in 1941, Tito played a big role in the resistance. In 1953, he became president for nearly 30 years. Unlike the rest of the Eastern bloc, Yugoslavia maintained its independence from the USSR. His government forced the different ethnic groups of the country to live together. Less than a decade after his death, the different areas of Yugoslavia separated into Macedonia, Serbia, Montenegro, Bosnia and Herzegovina, and became involved in a long and bitter civil war for territory and power.

**Trotsky, Leon (1879-1940)**
Russian revolutionary. As leader of the victorious Red Army during the Civil War, Trotsky was a powerful figure among Russian communists. In a power struggle following Lenin's death, Trotsky was defeated by Stalin and exiled. He continued to criticize Stalin and was murdered in 1940 in Mexico, probably by a Stalinist agent.

**Turing, Alan (1912-1954)**
British mathematician. During the Second World War, Turing designed the first practical computer program in order to crack secret German codes. His work was vital in the eventual Allied victory. After the war, he continued his crucial work in the development of computers. He also designed the Turing Test, which is used to test the intelligence of machines. He committed suicide partly because he was persecuted for his homosexuality.

**Walesa, Lech (1943- )**
Polish trade unionist. In 1980, Walesa, an electrician, led a shipworkers' strike in Poland. He went on to form an independent trade union called Solidarity which challenged the Polish government. In 1989, the first free elections for over 40 years were held in Poland, and Solidarity easily won. Walesa later became president of the new republic.

**Warhol, Andy (1927-1987)**
US artist. During the 1960s, Warhol became the best known of the pop artists. He took everyday objects, such as soup cans and coke bottles, and used them as repeated images in his art. From 1965, he spent more time directing films in which nothing ever happened, and managing rock groups.

**Welles, Orson (1915-85)**
US film director. After a successful career producing and directing radio plays, Welles moved into cinema. In 1941, he wrote, directed, produced and starred in his first film *Citizen Kane*, a grand epic about the life and death of a newspaper owner. Critics loved it, but it was difficult to live up to. He went on to direct various adaptations of Shakespeare plays, and act in films directed by others, but he never matched his early glory.

**Williams, Tennessee (1911-1983)**
US playwright. Plays such as *The Glass Menagerie* (1945) and *A Streetcar named Desire* (1947) were concerned with madness, weakness and fear, often in women. By examining the hidden side of life and people's repressions, Williams changed the nature of playwriting and the way that we view the deep South of the USA, where many of his plays are set.

**Wittgenstein, Ludwig (1889-1951)**
Philosopher. Wittgenstein's two major works *Tractus Logico-Philosophicus* (1922) and *Philosophical Investigations* (1953) both had a great influence on modern thought. By analyzing the links between logic, philosophy and language, he pioneered an approach that became very popular.

**Yeltsin, Boris (1931- )**
Russian president. When Mikhail Gorbachev was deposed in a military coup in 1991, Yeltsin, the Russian prime minister, took control and helped to crush the coup. When the USSR broke up, Yeltsin became president of Russia, the biggest state.

**Zapata, Emiliano (1879-1919)**
Mexican revolutionary. In 1911, Zapata led a revolution against the Mexican dictator Porfiro Diaz. He wanted the Mexican people to claim back their land from the imperial Spanish landowners. Zapata continued to fight for control of Mexico, but was assassinated in 1919. He became a symbol of Latin American resistance.

# Date chart 1900-50

| | INTERNATIONAL POLITICS | DOMESTIC POLITICS |
|---|---|---|

## 1900s

**INTERNATIONAL POLITICS**

1900 Boxer Rebellion in China against foreign powers.
1902 Boer War ends.
Panama gains independence from Colombia.
1903 Russo-Japanese War begins.
1905 Norway gains independence from Sweden.

**DOMESTIC POLITICS**

1900 King of Italy is assassinated by anarchist.
1901 US president, McKinley, is assassinated.
1902 Portugal goes bankrupt.
1905 Sinn Fein is founded in Ireland.
1908 King and prince of Portugal are assassinated.

## 1910s

**INTERNATIONAL POLITICS**

1911 Italy and Turkey at war
1912 First Balkan War
1913 Second Balkan War
1914 First World War begins.
1915 Italy joins Allies.
1916 Battles of Somme and Verdun
1917 US declares war on Germany.
German and Russian peace at Brest-Litovsk
British politician Balfour supports Jewish homeland in the Balfour Declaration.
1918 Allies make peace with Austria, then Germany.
President Wilson issues 14 points for peace.
1919 Treaty of Versailles

**DOMESTIC POLITICS**

1910 Revolution in Portugal
Young Turk rebellion in Turkey
1911 Russian and Spanish prime ministers are assassinated.
Revolution in Mexico
1912 Manchu dynasty abdicates in China.
1913 King of Greece and Mexican president are assassinated.
1916 Easter rising takes place in Dublin.
1917 Russian revolution
1918 Russian empire is renamed USSR and Tsar Nicholas and his family are executed.
1919 Mussolini founds fascist party.
Hitler founds Nazi party.

## 1920s

**INTERNATIONAL POLITICS**

1920 First meeting of League of Nations
1921 Turks win war against Greece.
Paris peace conference fixes German war reparations.
1923 France occupies Ruhr region of Germany.
1925 French troops begin to withdraw from Rhineland.
1927 Albania makes defensive treaty with Italy.
1929 Wall Street Crash in USA leads to worldwide economic depression.

**DOMESTIC POLITICS**

1922 Civil war in Ireland
Mussolini becomes Italian prime minister.
1923 Ataturk becomes first president of Turkey.
1920 First meeting of League of Nations
1924 Lenin dies.
1925 Fascists become only party in Italy.
Hitler's book *Mein Kampf* published.
1926 Hejaz's name changes to Saudi Arabia.
General Strike in Britain
1927 First Five Year Plan in USSR

## 1930s

**INTERNATIONAL POLITICS**

1931 Japan invades Manchuria.
1935 Saar region is restored to German control.
Italy invades Abyssinia.
1936 China declares war on Japan.
1938 Austria is declared part of German Reich.
Nazi troops occupy part of Czechoslovakia.
Libya is declared part of Italy.
1939 Germany invades Poland.
Britain and France declare war on Germany, marking the start of the Second World War.
Russia invades Finland.

**DOMESTIC POLITICS**

1930 Gandhi begins campaign of civil disobedience.
1931 Revolution in Spain, king is deposed.
1932 French president is assassinated.
1933 Hitler becomes German Chancellor.
Persecution of German Jews begins.
Roosevelt begins New Deal policies.
1934 Hitler is appointed Fuhrer.
Stalin begins purges.
1935 Germany reintroduces conscription.
1936 Germany occupies Rhineland.
Spanish Civil War begins.
1939 General Franco takes power in Spain.

## 1940s

**INTERNATIONAL POLITICS**

1940 Germany invades Norway, Denmark, Holland, Belgium, France and Luxembourg.
Italy declares war on Britain and France.
1941 Germany invades USSR.
Japan bombs Pearl Harbor.
Germany and Italy declare war on USA.
1942 Japan invades Burma and Dutch East Indies.
1943 Germans surrender at Stalingrad, USSR.
Italy surrenders.
1944 D-day landings in France
Paris and Brussels are liberated.
1945 Atomic bombs are dropped on Japan.
End of Second World War
1946 First meeting of UN assembly
1947 Marshall plan starts.
1949 NATO and the Council of Europe form.

**DOMESTIC POLITICS**

1940 Trotsky is assassinated in Mexico.
1943 Rationing begins on meat, fat and cheese in the USA.
Huge Jewish uprising in Warsaw, Poland
1945 President Roosevelt dies.
1946 Albanian King Zog deposed and a republic is declared.
1947 India, Pakistan and Burma become independent.
1948 Gandhi assassinated.
State of Israel is declared.
1949 Mao Zedong becomes president of China.
Eire (southern Ireland) becomes a republic.
Apartheid begins in South Africa.
Indonesia and Vietnam become independent.

| SCIENCE AND INVENTION | ARTS | SPORTS AND GENERAL |
|---|---|---|
| 1900 Zepellin airship's first flight. Planck publishes work on quantum theory. | 1900 Puccini's opera *Tosca* first performed. | 1900 Olympic games in Paris |
| 1901 First motorbikes | 1904 *Peter Pan* written by J. M. Barrie | 1901 First Nobel prizes awarded. |
| 1903 Transatlantic radio messages First powered flight | Rodin sculpts *The Thinker*. Otto Wagner designs the | 1904 Olympics in St. Louis, USA |
| 1908 Louis Blériot crosses English Channel in a plane. | Postal Savings Bank, Vienna. 1907 First exhibition of Cubist paintings in Paris. | 1906 Nightwork by women is internationally forbidden. 1907 Boy scout movement founded. 1908 Olympic games in London 1909 Girl guide movement founded. |
| 1910 Plastics are invented. | 1910 Wasily Kandinsky paints first abstract painting. | 1911 Norwegian team led by Roald Amundsen reaches |
| 1912 Cellophane is manufactured. | 1911 Irving Berlin composes | the South Pole. |
| 1913 Assembly line production is introduced. Neils Bohr builds model of structure of the atom. | *Alexander's Ragtime Band.* Cubists start using collage. 1913 Proust writes *Swann's Way.* Shaw writes *Pygmalion.* | 1912 Titanic hits iceberg and sinks, taking 1513 lives. Olympic games in Stockholm Charles Pathe produces the first newsreel. |
| 1915 Poison gas is used by Germans | Stravinsky composes *The Rite* | 1914 Panama Canal opens to sea |
| 1916 First tanks are used | *of Spring.* | traffic. |
| 1917 Carl Jung publishes *The Psychology of the Unconscious.* | Chaplin makes his first film. 1916 Dada movement begins. 1917 First jazz record issued. | 1918 Vote is given to women over 30 in Britain. |
| 1919 Alcock and Brown make first non-stop Atlantic flight. | 1919 Bauhaus School founded. Film *Cabinet of Doctor Caligari.* | 1919 Great Spanish 'flu epidemic |
| 1920 Gramophone records are recorded electronically | 1922 James Joyce publishes *Ulysses.* 1924 George Gershwin composes | 1920 US women get the vote. Joan of Arc made a saint. |
| 1922 Insulin is developed as a treatment for diabetes. | *Rhapsody in Blue.* 1925 Kafka writes *The Trial.* | US Prohibition introduced. 1921 First footprints of the Yeti |
| 1923 First helicopter flight | Sergei Eisenstein directs film | reported in Himalayas. |
| 1925 First traffic light is used. | *Battleship Potemkin.* | 1922 Howard Carter discovers |
| 1926 Baird invents the television. | 1927 First full length talking film | Tutankhamen's tomb. |
| 1927 Lindbergh flies solo across the Atlantic. | *The Jazz Singer* First Oscars are awarded. | First cocktail shaken. 1924 Olympic games in Paris |
| 1928 Fleming discovers penicillin. | 1928 First *Mickey Mouse* cartoon | 1928 Olympic games in Amsterdam |
| 1930 Planet Pluto is sighted. Amy Johnson flies solo from Britain to Australia. | 1930 Empire State Building, New York, completed. 1933 Lorca's *Blood Wedding* first | 1930 First World Cup soccer tournament held, and won by Uruguay. |
| 1932 Vitamin D discovered. Jansky pioneers radio astronomy. | performed. 1934 Riefenstahl directs *Triumph of the Will.* | 1932 Olympic games in Los Angeles 1933 Prohibition ends in USA. 1936 Berlin Olympics used as a |
| 1933 Polythene developed. 1934 The Cat's Eye road reflector is invented. | 1936 *Gone with the Wind* written by Margaret Mitchell. 1937 Picasso paints *Guernica.* | showcase for the Third Reich and Hitler's theory of racial superiority. |
| 1937 Whittle makes first jet engine. 1938 Ladislo Biro invents ballpoint pen. | 1939 *Gone with the Wind* made, which becomes one of most successful films ever. | 1937 The world's largest airship, *The Hindenburg,* burst into flames and was destroyed. |
| 1940 Penicillin is developed as an antibiotic. | 1941 Orson Welles directs, writes and stars in *Citizen Kane.* | 1945 French women are given the vote for first time. |
| 1941 Manhattan project begins. | 1943 Film *Casablanca* is released. | 1946 Italian women are given the |
| 1942 Magnetic tape is invented. Americans develop ENIAC, the first automatic computer. Germans launch *V-2* rocket. | 1945 George Orwell publishes *Animal Farm.* Carlo Levi publishes *Christ stopped at Eboli.* | vote. US supreme court rules that segregation on buses is illegal. Joe Louis successfully defends |
| 1944 First kidney machine developed. | 1947 Tenessee Williams' *A Streetcar Named Desire* is performed. | boxing heavyweight title for 23rd time. |
| 1945 Atomic bomb is dropped and effects of radiation realized. | Le Corbusier designs *Unité d'habitation.* | 1948 Belgian women get the vote. First Olympic games for 12 |
| 1947 First supersonic flight 1948 LPs and transistor radios are invented. | 1948 De Sica directs *The Bicycle Thieves.* 1949 Simone de Beauvoir publishes | years held in London. First World Health Assembly held in Geneva. |
| 1949 Cortisone is discovered. | *The Second Sex.* | |

# Date chart from 1950

| | INTERNATIONAL POLITICS | DOMESTIC POLITICS |
|---|---|---|

## 1950s

**INTERNATIONAL POLITICS**

| | |
|---|---|
| 1950 | China invades Tibet. |
| | North Korea invades South Korea. |
| | USA sends military mission to Vietnam. |
| 1954 | USA sends troops to Vietnam. |
| 1955 | Italy, Germany and France form European Union. |
| 1956 | Egypt seizes Suez Canal. |
| | Britain and France send troops to Suez. |
| | Soviet troops invade Hungary to put down anti-Soviet uprising. |
| 1957 | European Common Market begins. |

**DOMESTIC POLITICS**

| | |
|---|---|
| 1950 | Anti-communism becomes political force in USA. |
| 1953 | Stalin dies. |
| 1954 | Nasser seizes power in Egypt. |
| 1955 | South Vietnam is declared part of republic of Vietnam. |
| 1956 | Sudan and Morocco become independent. |
| 1957 | Tunisia is made a republic. |
| | Ghana becomes independent. |
| 1958 | State of Alaska joins the USA. |
| 1959 | Castro comes to power in Cuba. |

## 1960s

**INTERNATIONAL POLITICS**

| | |
|---|---|
| 1961 | Cuban exiles stage Bay of Pigs invasion. |
| | Berlin Wall is built. |
| 1962 | Cuban missile crisis |
| | Soviet-Cuban trade treaty is signed. |
| 1964 | A UN peace force takes control in Cyprus. |
| 1965 | War breaks out between India and Pakistan. |
| 1967 | Six-day war between Israel and Arab nations. |
| 1968 | Czechoslovakia is invaded by Soviet troops. |
| 1969 | First US troops are withdrawn from Vietnam, partly as a result of massive anti-Vietnam protest across the USA. |

**DOMESTIC POLITICS**

| | |
|---|---|
| 1960 | Cyprus and the Congo become independent. |
| | US Senate safeguards African-American rights. |
| 1962 | Uganda and Tanganyika become independent. |
| 1963 | J.F. Kennedy is assassinated in Dallas, Texas, USA. |
| | Kenya becomes independent. |
| 1964 | Tanzania and Zambia are founded. |
| | Malta and Malawi become independent. |
| 1965 | Revolution in Algeria. |
| 1966 | Cultural revolution begins in China. |
| | Guyana becomes independent. |
| 1967 | King of Greece is exiled after coup. |
| 1968 | Student and worker revolts in Paris in May. |

## 1970s

**INTERNATIONAL POLITICS**

| | |
|---|---|
| 1971 | Fighting in Indochina spreads to Laos and Cambodia. |
| 1973 | Britain, Eire and Denmark become members of the EEC |
| | Full ceasefire in Vietnam |
| | Yom Kippur War is fought between Israel and Arab countries |
| 1974 | Worldwide inflation and financial depression |
| 1976 | French plane kidnapped by Palestinian group at Entebbe, Uganda. |
| 1978 | USA and China re-establish diplomatic relations. |
| 1979 | Israel and Egypt sign peace treaty in Washington |
| | Soviet Union invades Afghanistan. |

**DOMESTIC POLITICS**

| | |
|---|---|
| 1970 | Nigerian Civil War ends. |
| 1971 | Idi Amin seizes power in Uganda. |
| 1972 | Bangladesh becomes separate state. |
| | Watergate scandal in USA |
| 1973 | Military coup in Chile |
| 1975 | Civil War in Angola, Ethiopia and Lebanon |
| | Mozambique becomes independent. |
| | Monarchy is restored in Spain when Franco dies. |
| 1976 | Mao Zedong, ruler of China, dies. |
| 1978 | Somalia and the Solomons become independent. |
| | Coup in Afghanistan |
| 1979 | Iranian revolution, Shah of Iran is deposed. |
| | Rhodesia is renamed Zimbabwe. |

## 1980s

**INTERNATIONAL POLITICS**

| | |
|---|---|
| 1980 | 100,000s of Soviet troops are airlifted into Afghanistan. |
| 1981 | Greece joins the EEC. |
| 1982 | Argentina invades the Falkland Islands and war breaks out between Argentina and Britain. |
| 1983 | The USA invades Grenada. |
| 1986 | Spain and Portugal join the EEC. |
| 1987 | International stock market collapses. |
| | Reagan and Gorbachev sign arms reduction treaty between USA and USSR. |
| 1989 | Soviet troops leave Afghanistan. |

**DOMESTIC POLITICS**

| | |
|---|---|
| 1980 | Polish workers strike and seize Gdansk shipyard. |
| | Ronald Reagan becomes president of USA. |
| 1981 | US president, Reagan, is shot but not killed. |
| | Egyptian president, Sadat, is assassinated. |
| | Pope John Paul II is shot but not killed. |
| 1984 | Indira Gandhi is assassinated. |
| 1987 | Irangate scandal in USA |
| 1989 | Tiananmen Square massacre in China. |
| 1989 | Berlin Wall is demolished. |
| | Civil War in Romania, Ceausescu is deposed. |

## 1990s

**INTERNATIONAL POLITICS**

| | |
|---|---|
| 1990 | Iraq invades Kuwait. |
| | US troops are sent to Gulf. |
| | Declaration of the end of the Cold War is signed in Paris. |
| 1991 | Gulf War between Iraq and Allied forces. |
| | Warsaw pact is dissolved. |
| | Slovenia and Croatia declare independence from Yugoslavia. |
| 1992 | Bosnia and Hercegovina vote for independence from Yugoslavia |
| 1993 | Israel and the PLO enter peace negotiations. |

**DOMESTIC POLITICS**

| | |
|---|---|
| 1990 | Nelson Mandela is released in South Africa. |
| | Namibia is made independent. |
| | Gorbachev is awarded Nobel Peace prize. |
| | East and West Germany are unified. |
| 1991 | President de Klerk promises end of apartheid. |
| | Military coup in USSR. |
| | Final break-up of the USSR |
| 1992 | Czechoslovakia breaks up into the Czech Republic and Slovakia. |
| 1993 | Political battles between Yeltsin and opponents, leads to fighting and death of 500 people. |

## SCIENCE AND INVENTION

1952 US explodes first hydrogen bomb.
First contraceptive pill
1953 Crick and Watson discover structure of DNA.
1954 Link between lung cancer and smoking is first suggested.
First vertical take-off plane
1955 Polio vaccine is discovered.
1957 USSR launch unmanned spacecraft *Sputnik*.
1958 Stereo records become available.

1960 First cardiac pacemaker
1961 First person in space
1962 Telstar satellite is launched.
US astronauts are put in orbit.
1963 Vaccine for measles discovered
1965 Soviet and US astronauts walk in space.
1966 Soviet and US craft land on moon.
1967 First heart transplant
1969 Two US astronauts walk on the moon.

1970 First solar furnace paves way for more use of solar energy
1973 Computerized X-ray scanning is developed.
First space station *Skylab* launched.
1976 Concorde makes first commercial transatlantic flight.
1977 US space shuttle makes test flight.
1978 World's very first test-tube baby is born.

1981 US launches first space shuttle, *Columbia*.
1982 First artificial heart is fitted.
AIDS is first identified.
1984 US astronauts walk in space without being attached to a craft.
1986 US space shuttle *Challenger* explodes.
1989 *Voyager 2* spacecraft takes pictures of Neptune.

1990 Scientists discover that ozone layer is thinning faster than had been thought.
1991 New astronomical discoveries call into question theories on the origin of the universe.
New contraceptive, which places tubes under women's skin, is approved.
1992 New meningitus vaccine is introduced.

## ARTS

1950 Le Corbusier designs Chapel at Ronchamp, France.
1951 J D Salinger publishes *The Catcher in the Rye*.
1954 Kurosawa directs *The Seven Samurai*.
1956 Utzon designs the Sydney Opera House.
Frank Lloyd Wright designs Guggenheim Museum, New York.
Bergman films *The Seventh Seal*.
1958 Pasternak writes *Dr Zhivago*.

1960 Jean Luc Godard directs *A Bout de Souffle*.
Hitchcock directs *Psycho*.
1961 *West Side Story* is performed.
1963 Solzhenitsyn publishes *One Day in the Life of Ivan Denisovich*.
Fellini directs *8½*.
Lichtenstein paints *Whaam!*
1967 The Beatles release *Sergeant Pepper Lonely Hearts Club Band*
1968 Kubrick directs *2001: Space Odyssey*.

1971 Kubrick directs *A Clockwork Orange*.
1972 Francis Ford Coppola directs *The Godfather*.
1975 Film *One Flew over the Cuckoo's Nest* is released.
1976 Garcia Marquez publishes *The Autumn of the Patriarch*
1977 *Star Wars* becomes the top grossing film to date.
1978 Isaac Bashevis Singer wins Nobel Prize for Literature.

1980 Umberto Eco publishes *The Name of the Rose*.
1982 *ET* becomes top grossing film.
G G Marquez publishes *Chronicle of a Death Foretold*.
1985 Live Aid music concert in Britain and the USA raises $70 million for Africa.
1988 Salman Rushdie's *Satanic Verses* published and declared blasphemous by Muslims.

1990 Paris' new Bastille Opera is opened.
1992 Freddie Mercury of Queen dies.
1993 *Jurassic Park* becomes top grossing film.
*Cheers*, the USA's most popular TV comedy, ends.
Writer Toni Morrison wins Nobel Prize for Literature.
*Usborne History of the 20th Century* is published.

## SPORTS AND GENERAL

1951 US couple, the Rosenbergs, are found guilty of spying for USSR and are executed.
1952 Helsinki Olympics
1953 Mount Everest is climbed for first time ever.
1954 Bannister runs first four minute mile.
1956 Melbourne Olympics
1958 Women priests ordained in some US and Swedish Christian churches.

1960 Rome Olympics
1962 Many children are born with malformations due to the use of the drug *thalidomide* in pregnancy.
1964 Tokyo Olympics
1966 Soccer World cup trophy stolen, but later found by dog in a London park.
1968 Mexico Olympics
1969 Huge open-air music festival in Woodstock, USA

1971 Women get the vote in Switzerland.
1972 Earthquakes in Nicaragua
Munich Olympics shadowed by the killing of 11 Israeli athletes by Arab terrorists.
1976 Montreal Olympics
Earthquake in Italy
1977 USA restores the death penalty
1978 Three popes in one year.
900 members of a religious cult commit suicide in Guyana.

1980 Moscow Olympics boycotted by Germany, USA and Kenya.
1984 Bhopal disaster in India
Los Angeles Olympics boycotted by Communist countries.
1985 Earthquake in Mexico City
1986 Chernobyl nuclear meltdown in USSR
1988 Seoul Olympics
1989 *Exxon Valdez* oil spill

1990 Breakthrough is made in Channel Tunnel.
1992 Barcelona Olympics
First UN environmental summit held in Brazil.
1996 Olympics in Atlanta, USA
2000 Olympics in Sydney, Australia

# Index

In this index, some page numbers beside place names are in italics. This indicates that the place features on a map.

The publishers are grateful to the following organizations for permission to reproduce their material, or to use it as artist's reference:

Apple Corps, London, 55 (Beatles)
Amnesty International, London, 75 (poster, symbol, El Salvador)
Associated Press, London, 59
Collection of Lord and Lady Briggs, 3
BT Museum (UK), 63 (Kennedy)
Cavendish Laboratory, Cambridge, 37 (Crick)
Crown Copyright (UK), 63 (weather)
EC (UK), 67
Genesis Space Photos, cover, 65
Health Education Authority, London, 37 (AIDS poster)
Hulton Deutsch Collection, London, 2 (Pi Yu), 6, 10, 11, 13 (Romanov), 16, 25, 38, 40, 41 (Smith), 42, 43 (Arafat), 47 (Brezhnev and Solzhenitsyn), 48 (Kennedy), 50 (Eisenhower), 51 (King), 57 (Castro), 60, 61, 66, 68 (Walesa), 74, 75 (Gandhi), 79
Hulton Deutsch/Bettmann, 50 (Kennedy)
Hulton Deutsch/Reuters 50 (Nixon)
Magnum, London, 47 (Czech poster)
Mary Evans, London, cover, 24
Novosti, London, 68 (Gorbachev)
Pictorial, London, cover (Beatles) 54, 55 (Madonna, Marley, Jukebox)

Popperfoto, Northampton, 2 (Yeltsin), 7, 9, 32, 34, 39, 41 (Mandela), 43 (Camp David), 48 (Ho Chi Minh and Cuban missile sites), 51 (Reagan), 52 (Dali), 56, 57 (North), 70, 71, 73
St. Mary's Hospital Medical School, 36
SCRSS, 12, 13 (cartoon)
Ullstein Bilderdienst, 22, 23

The works of art listed below are reproduced by kind permission of the following organizations:

*Rabbit*, 1986, Jeff Koons. Saatchi Collection, London
*Family Group*, Henry Moore © Henry Moore Foundation 1993. Reproduced by kind permission of the Henry Moore Foundation
*Guernica*, 1937, Pablo Picasso, © DACS 1993, Prado Museum, Madrid
*The Three Dancers*, 1925, Pablo Picasso © DACS 1993, Tate Gallery, London
*Marilyn X 100*, 1962, Andy Warhol, © Andy Warhol Foundation, New York. Saatchi Collection.

Every effort has been made to trace the copyright holders of material in this book. If any rights have been omitted, the publishers offer their apologies and will rectify this in any subsequent editions following notification.

To be continued...